WHO ARE THE TERRORISTS?

THE ROOTS OF TERRORISM

WHO ARE THE TERRORISTS?

Dipak K. Gupta

San Diego State University

Series Consulting Editors

Leonard Weinberg and William L. Eubank

University of Nevada, Reno

CHELSEA HOUSE
PUBLISHERS
An imprint of Infobase Publishing

This book is dedicated to
Sudip, Arman, Shalini, Devraj, Jaya, Sumana, Ayesha, Ishan,
Ritam, Jeet, Rohini, Nainika, Rusha, and Trina.
The young adults and soon to be.

_____

Who Are the Terrorists?

Copyright © 2006 by Infobase Publishing

Chelsea House
An imprint of Infobase Publishing
132 West 31st Street
New York NY 10001

Library of Congress Cataloging-in-Publication Data

Gupta, Dipak K.
  Who are the terrorists?/Dipak K. Gupta.
    p. cm.—(The roots of terrorism)
  Includes bibliographical references and index.
ISBN 0-7910-8306-3 (hard cover)
  1. Terrorism. 2. Terrorists—Psychology. 3. Terrorism—Prevention. I. Title. II. Series.
HV6431.G858 2005
303.6'25—dc22   2005021627

Chelsea House books are available at special discounts when purchased in bulk quantities for businesses, associations, institutions, or sales promotions. Please call our Special Sales Department in New York at (212) 967-8800 or (800) 322-8755.

You can find Chelsea House on the World Wide Web at http://www.chelseahouse.com

Text and cover design by Takeshi Takahashi

Printed in the United States of America

Bang 21C 10 9 8 7 6 5 4 3 2

This book is printed on acid-free paper.

All links and web addresses were checked and verified to be correct at the time of publication. Because of the dynamic nature of the web, some addresses and links may have changed since publication and may no longer be valid.

WHO ARE THE TERRORISTS?

Dipak K. Gupta

San Diego State University

Series Consulting Editors

Leonard Weinberg and William L. Eubank

University of Nevada, Reno

CHELSEA HOUSE
P U B L I S H E R S

An imprint of Infobase Publishing

*This book is dedicated to
Sudip, Arman, Shalini, Devraj, Jaya, Sumana, Ayesha, Ishan,
Ritam, Jeet, Rohini, Nainika, Rusha, and Trina.
The young adults and soon to be.*

———

Who Are the Terrorists?

Copyright © 2006 by Infobase Publishing

Chelsea House
An imprint of Infobase Publishing
132 West 31st Street
New York NY 10001

Library of Congress Cataloging-in-Publication Data

Gupta, Dipak K.
   Who are the terrorists?/Dipak K. Gupta.
      p. cm.—(The roots of terrorism)
   Includes bibliographical references and index.
   ISBN 0-7910-8306-3 (hard cover)
    1. Terrorism. 2. Terrorists—Psychology. 3. Terrorism—Prevention. I. Title. II. Series.
HV6431.G858 2005
303.6'25—dc22   2005021627

Chelsea House books are available at special discounts when purchased in bulk quantities for businesses, associations, institutions, or sales promotions. Please call our Special Sales Department in New York at (212) 967-8800 or (800) 322-8755.

You can find Chelsea House on the World Wide Web at http://www.chelseahouse.com

Text and cover design by Takeshi Takahashi

Printed in the United States of America

Bang 21C 10 9 8 7 6 5 4 3 2

This book is printed on acid-free paper.

All links and web addresses were checked and verified to be correct at the time of publication. Because of the dynamic nature of the web, some addresses and links may have changed since publication and may no longer be valid.

Leonard Weinberg and William L. Eubank
University of Nevada, Reno

Terrorism is hard to ignore. Almost every day television news shows, newspapers, magazines, and Websites run and re-run pictures of dramatic and usually bloody acts of violence carried out by ferocious-looking terrorists or claimed by shadowy militant groups. It is often hard not to be scared when we see people like us killed or maimed by terrorist attacks at fast food restaurants, in office buildings, on public buses and trains, or along normal-looking streets.

This kind of fear is exactly what those staging terrorist attacks hope to achieve. They want the public, especially the American public, to feel a profound sense of fear. Often the leaders of terrorist groups want the public not only to be frightened by the attack, but also angry at the government because it seems unable to protect them from these violent assaults.

This series of books for young people has two related purposes. The first is to place the events we see in context. We want young readers to know what terrorism is about: Who its perpetrators are, where they come from, and what they hope to gain by their violence. We also want to answer some basic questions about this type of violence: What is terrorism? What do we mean when we use the term? Is one man's terrorist another man's freedom fighter? Is terrorism new, a kind of asymmetrical warfare just invented at the beginning of the twenty-first century? Or, does terrorism have a long history stretching back over the centuries? Does terrorism ever end? Should we expect to face waves of terrorist violence stretching into the indefinite future?

This series' second purpose is to reduce the anxieties and fears of young readers. Getting a realistic picture of what terrorism is all about, knowing what is true and what is not true about it helps us "get a grip." Young readers will learn, we hope, what constitutes realistic concerns about the danger of terrorism versus irrational fear. By understanding the nature of the threat, we help defeat one of the terrorists' basic aims: spreading terror.

The first volume in the series, *What is Terrorism?*, by Leonard Weinberg and William L. Eubank, begins by defining the term "terrorism," then goes on to explain the immediate aims and long-term objectives of those who decide to use this unconventional form of violence. Weinberg and Eubank point out that terrorism did not begin with the 9/11 attacks on the United States. In fact, terrorist violence has a long history, one the authors trace from its religious roots in the ancient Middle East up to current times.

For those who believe that terrorist campaigns, once started, are endless, Jeffrey Ian Ross's *Will Terrorism End?* will come as a useful antidote. Ross calls our attention to the various ways in which terrorist episodes have ended in the past. Many readers will be surprised to learn that most of the terrorist organizations that were active in Latin America, Western Europe, and the United States just a few decades ago have passed from the scene. For example, the Irish Republican Army (IRA), long active in paramilitary operations in Northern Ireland, is now in the process of turning to peaceful political participation.

Between accounts of the beginning and end of terrorism are books that approach the problem in two different ways. Dipak K. Gupta (*Who are the Terrorists?*) and Assaf Moghadam (*The Roots of Terrorism*) answer general questions about the origins of terrorists and terrorist organizations. Gupta provides profiles of individual terrorists and terrorist groups, in addition to exploring the issues that inspire terrorists. Moghadam, on the other hand, is more concerned with the organizational and social roots of terrorism. For example: What causes people to join terrorist groups? What are the grievances that often give rise to terrorist campaigns?

While Gupta and Moghadam examine the roots of terrorism in general terms, Jack Levin and Arie Perliger's books each have a specific geographic focus. Levin's *Domestic Terrorism* brings the story close to home by describing domestic terrorist activity in the United States over the last half century. Perliger's book, *Middle Eastern Terrorism*, offers an account of terrorist activity in the region of the world with which such violence is most closely identified.

Finally, we believe that young readers will come away from this series of books with a much clearer understanding of what terrorism is and what those individuals and groups who carry out terrorist attacks are like. ∎

There is a story of a fabled emperor in India who asked the wise men of his court, "Which is the most common profession?" Since there was no census, nobody knew the answer. Only the court jester spoke up, "The physicians."

"Really?" The amazed emperor turned to the man, "Prove it."

The next day, the court jester went to the main market and pretended to have a terrible stomach pain. Seeing his discomfort, everybody came over and offered advice. "See, your Majesty, every-one is a doctor," said the court jester, recounting his story to the emperor, offering his proof.

The court jester had a point: Since good health is important to everybody, to become a doctor (or to dispense medical advise) comes naturally to all of us. Similarly, in the aftermath of the September 11, 2001, terrorist attacks, each of us had to become an expert on terrorism. Suddenly, terrorism was everybody's business. Yet, like a lot of folk medicine, people's knowledge of terrorism can be based on prejudice, presupposition, and misconceptions. For about a quarter century, a great deal of effort has gone into terrorism research. Since the threat of international terrorism is not likely to decrease anytime soon, it is important to get an accurate picture of the causes of terrorism and who the terrorists are.

Most of us did not think much about terrorism before September 11, 2001. Unconcerned, we Americans were going about our lives as we always did. On the other side of the world, in the dusty caves of remote Afghanistan, a group of terrorists hatched an elaborate plan to strike the United States and inflict such harm that we would always remember their hatred for us.

Every generation defines its time based on some momentous event. Those who were alive at the time remember VE Day, May 8, 1945, when the forces of Nazi Germany unconditionally surrendered. Those who were old enough to remember would always recall the exact moment they heard the awful news that an assassin's bullets had taken the life of President John F. Kennedy on November 22, 1963. Similarly, the images of airplanes crashing into the Twin Towers of the World Trade Center and people jumping from the skyscrapers on 9/11 will forever be seared into our memories.

The attacks of September 11, 2001, took the lives of nearly 3,000 people and altered the course of history. After the initial shock was over, the entire nation wanted to know: Who are these terrorists and why do they hate us so? Seemingly overnight, terrorism was everyone's concern. By using the work of scholars and terrorism experts, we hope to discover in this book who the terrorists really are: What motivates them? What do terrorists want to accomplish by their acts? How should we deal with the ever-growing threat of terrorism?

In this book, I raise a number of important questions that are most commonly asked about terrorists and their groups, and present evidence found in the scholarly literature. Readers can then use this information to come up with their own responses. I hope this book can elevate the level of discussion to one based on facts, and not on prejudice.

Before we start, I would like you take a quiz about terrorism and terrorists. I would like you to answer these questions to the best of your knowledge. After you have finished the book, I would like you to answer the questions once again and see if you have changed your mind. For many of these questions there is no strictly "right" or "wrong" answer. So, as you compare your responses, you can see whether or not you find any reason to change your mind about them.

Terrorism Quiz

Are the following statements true or false?

We know how to define terrorism.	True/False
Terrorism is a recent phenomenon in history.	True/False
Terrorists are considered as evil people throughout history.	True/False
All terrorists are Muslim.	True/False
All terrorists are inspired by ideology.	True/False
All terrorists are crazy or "brainwashed."	True/False
All suicide terrorists are of Middle Eastern origin.	True/False
Terrorist are uneducated people with little hope for success in life.	True/False
All terrorists belong to strong, hierarchical groups.	True/False
All terrorists are young and male.	True/False
The only way to deal with terrorism is to hit them hard militarily.	True/False
I could never be a terrorist and kill innocent men, women, and children.	True/False

CHAPTER 1

WHAT IS TERRORISM?

The term *terrorism* originated during to the French Revolution. From the beginning, the word had different meanings for different people. The French Revolution was the result of the French aristocracy's social and economic oppression of the common people. On July 14, 1789, the people of Paris stormed the most hated symbol of oppression, the Bastille prison, and destroyed it brick by brick. Just as we celebrate the Fourth of July as the beginning of the American Revolution, so the people of France celebrate Bastille Day, which marked the beginning of the French Revolution.

Yet, after achieving power, the French Revolution started to consume itself. On July 26, 1794, the revolutionary leader Maximilien Robespierre announced to the National Convention that he had in

As a method of execution, the guillotine, shown above, was thought to be quicker—and thus more humane—than the older forms of beheading by sword or hanging. Because of its use during the Reign of Terror, however, it came to symbolize the horror of a revolution gone terribly wrong.

his possession a list of names of traitors who were plotting to overthrow the revolutionary government. Thus started the "Reign of Terror," during which nearly 40,000 men and women were publicly beheaded by the use of the guillotine.[1] These gruesome acts were carried out in order to instill fear in the minds of the "enemies" of the revolution and to assure the common people that the old, unjust system of monarchy was not going to return. So, if you were an aristocrat or wanted to restore the monarchy, these acts were designed to terrify you into submission. If, on the other hand, you were a commoner and a supporter of the revolution, these were viewed as necessary acts to bring about a new French society. The feared prosecutor Georges Danton proclaimed, "Let us be terrible, so that people will not have to be."[2]

This was the origin of the term *terrorism*, which from its very birth combined violence with the theater of a public spectacle. Thus, terrorism is considered "propaganda by deed" (a phrase coined by the noted Russian anarchist Peter Kropotkin): a form of mass communication by which a terrorist group tells its supporters, "we are doing it for you," while warning their enemies of the consequences of ignoring their demands.[3] Terrorism, therefore, will mean very different things to different people.

During the French Revolution, the direct impact of the public beheadings was restricted to those who were close enough to witness them. Today, the world of television, the Internet, and mass communications has expanded the scope and impact of terrorist acts. Indeed, terrorism and the mass media work hand in hand. It is the job of the media to report newsworthy events and the most shocking events have the strongest appeal for the audience. This is also what the terrorists want: Through their horrifying acts they seek a world audience.

It is fairly obvious that the terms *terrorist* and *terrorism* have strong negative connotations. Therefore, the groups that are engaged in violent activities never call themselves terrorists. For instance, if you look at the names of terrorist groups, they use words such as "liberation," "revolution," "justice," and "jihad" (a righteous war) in their names, but not "terrorist." Not surprisingly, among their supporters, the terrorists are known as "freedom fighters," "liberators," and "martyrs."

There is no denying the fact that for our peace and security, we must control terrorism. However, if the world is to confront the threat of terrorism, it must first define the term. For example, every government in the world has signed the Geneva Accord, which protects prisoners of war from inhuman treatment. The world has also accepted the Universal Declaration of Human

Rights. Unfortunately, there is no universally acceptable definition of terrorism. Let us try to understand the reasons and see what kinds of problems there are.

The Sicarii:
The Terrorists of Antiquity

The man looked around the crowded marketplace for his victim. He steadied his nerves by silently praying while feeling the cold metal of the small concealed dagger against his body. He was on a mission. Unlike all the other people trying sell or buy in the busy market, he was not interested in material gains. He had an important job to do for his people and for his God. After some time, he found his man, the High Priest, who was cooperating with the Roman occupiers. He moved close to the eminent man and, after plunging his dagger into the priest's heart, he fled through the throng of horrified onlookers.

It was an unsettled time in Jerusalem. The powerful Roman army was in full control of the city. They were desecrating the temple, the holiest shrine in the Jewish religion, and defiling the ancient religion with the help of Jewish collaborators. The assassin belonged to a group called the "zealots" who were noted for their strict observance of Jewish laws. But among the common people, they were known as the Sicarii, or the "dagger men."

The onlookers were horrified not only because of the murder, but also because it would bring severe retaliation from the Romans on the entire Jewish population. But that was the purpose of these extremists—they wanted the compliant Jewish people to rise up against the Romans. In fact, in the first century A.D., at the beginning of the Jewish Revolt, the Sicarii, with the help of other zealots, gained access to Jerusalem and committed a series of atrocities in order to force the population to war. In one account, they destroyed the city's food supply so that the people would be forced to fight against the Roman siege instead of negotiating for peace. Finally, as the Jewish historian Josephus tells us, the Roman army took back Jerusalem and exterminated the Sicarii.

When there is a law that prohibits certain types of behavior, it does it with reference to three factors: the act itself, the actor (the person doing the act), and the motive. For example, every government forbids killing (an act), except when the state itself (the actor) imposes the death penalty. Also, it may be permissible to kill another person in self-defense (motive). Keep these three factors in mind while you think about the definition of terrorism using the following examples.

We can all agree that it was an act of terrorism when al Qaeda operatives killed nearly 3,000 innocent people in the 9/11 attacks. Now, is it terrorism because of the act or the actor? How about the motive? Let us examine each of these.

Does the killing of a civilian population qualify as terrorism? In our history, we have many examples of indiscriminate killing of civilians, particularly in times of war. Consider the bombing of Dresden, Germany. In 1941, when Europe was engulfed in World War II, Charles Portal of the British air staff advocated the bombing of entire cities and towns as an example of the Allies' fire power. Portal claimed that this awesome display of military might would quickly bring about the collapse of civilian morale in Germany. Air Marshall Arthur Harris of the Royal Air Force (RAF) agreed with Portal; when Harris became the head of the RAF Bomber Command in February 1942, he introduced a policy of "area bombing," where entire cities and towns were targeted for intensive bombardment. Not surprisingly, the Germans called it "terror bombing."

The plan by the RAF and the United States Air Force was to create a firestorm. This was achieved by dropping incendiary bombs filled with highly combustible chemicals, such as magnesium, phosphorus, or petroleum jelly (napalm), in clusters over a specific target. After the entire area caught fire, the intense heat would rapidly force the hot air to rise above the bombed area. Since this would create a vacuum, cold air would then rush in at ground level and everyone in the vicinity would be sucked into a gigantic fireball. This effect is well

The destroyed city of Dresden is shown here, beneath a sculpture called "The Goodness." The Allies conducted a sustained bombing campaign against the city to show a devastating example of their fire power.

known to firefighters, and frightens even the most experienced when they handle an extremely hot blaze. It is known as "backdraft."

The trouble with creating this effect on a city was that it required a large number of planes. Since all the important German cities were highly fortified with anti-aircraft guns, in 1945, Air Marshall Harris decided to create a firestorm in the medieval city of Dresden. Dresden offered an excellent target because it had no military significance and so was not heavily defended. Dresden had a population of 650,000. At that time, however, a large numbers of refugees, fleeing from the advancing Soviet Army, were flooding the streets of the city, swelling the number of civilians. On February 13, 1945, nearly 800 RAF bombers started bombing Dresden around the clock. During the next two days, the U.S. Air Force sent over 500 heavy bombers to follow the RAF attack. The city of Dresden was almost totally destroyed. The resulting firestorm killed thousands of men, women, and children. Germans claimed that it killed over 100,000 people, while the Allied sources put the figure at only a third of that total.

So, was it terrorism? The Germans have called it that, but you may argue that it really did not qualify as "terrorism" because it took place during the war. If you do so, you are excusing the killing of a large number of civilians only because of the timing.

Or you may argue that it is the actor that makes a difference. An act of "terrorism" must be carried out by a small group and not a government. Then consider the following case: On the evening of December 21, 1988, Pan Am Flight 103 exploded in midair high above Lockerbie, a small Scottish town. The incident killed 259 people on the plane and 11 people on the ground, who were simply at the wrong place at the wrong time. It was quickly revealed that agents of the Libyan government planted the bombs on the plane. The government of Libya, headed by President Muammar Qaddafi, was engaged in a long-running battle with the United States and Western European government over the accusation that Qaddafi was sponsoring terrorism. In 1986, the U.S. Air Force had bombed Tripoli, the capital of Libya, as a warning to stop their activities. It was discovered that the bombing of the Pan

Aum Shinrikyo: The Doomsday Group

The Tokyo subways are known for their overcrowding. In fact, the railway employs people who, after dutifully bowing, push passengers into the compartments so that the doors can close. On March 20, 1995, as a train was pulling into a station, a canister left in a corner started spewing deadly sarin gas. As panic set in, people gasping for air rushed toward the gates. The attack killed 12 and injured over 5,000 others. It was later found that if the perpetrators had not make some simple mistakes, the death and injury tolls would have been catastrophic.

The police quickly discovered the culprits: members of a religious group called Aum Shinrikyo. The name is a combination of *Aum*, which is a sacred Hindu sound, and *Shinrikyo*, a Japanese term meaning "supreme truth." Shoko Asahara, a near-blind, former owner of a traditional medicine and acupuncture shop, established this religious organization in 1987 by combining Buddhism, Hinduism, and Christianity along with a strong belief in the prophecies of the sixteenth-century astrologer Nostradamus. The members of this group, estimated to have numbered 20,000 at its peak, believed that Asahara was a reincarnation of Jesus Christ.

The group drew highly trained middle-class and upper-middle-class followers. For instance, Ikuo Hayashi, the person who devised this chemical bomb, was a trained physician. He was given a life sentence for his crime. The others, including Asahara, were also convicted and are still in prison. However, despite the best efforts of the Japanese and other world governments, the group is far from being totally disbanded. In 2004, the U.S. State Department included Aum Shinrikyo in its list of active terrorist groups.

Am jet was an act of retaliation by the Libyans. A lengthy investigation led to the extradition of two Libyan agents. In 2001, one of them, Abdelbaset Ali Mohmed al Megrahi, was found guilty of the charge of planting a bomb by a Scottish court in the Hague.

Was it terrorism? A recognized government did it. If you agree that this act should qualify as terrorism, then you should know that the United States government, through the Central Intelligence Agency, has also directly sponsored covert acts that have resulted in civilian deaths in many countries, such as Cuba, which is ruled by Fidel Castro.

Then, you may argue, we should not call such activities "terrorism" considering the fact that Castro is a ruthless communist dictator. If you do so, you will be basing your argument on the motive of an action. In other words, if the cause is noble, then it is not terrorism. Before and during World War II, there were a number of assassination attempts against Adolph Hitler. If any of them had succeeded, the world might have been able to avert the war. We certainly would not have condemned such an action. Yet, Hitler was extremely popular in Germany—millions of Germans adored him.[4] From their perspective, would not such an action have been considered an act of terrorism?

Confused? So are the experts. Alex Schmid, a noted expert on terrorism, spent over 100 pages in his book, *Political Terrorism*, examining different definitions of terrorism. Yet, he finally gave up looking for a definition that would be universally acceptable. As a result, after years of debate and thousands of deaths, we are still no closer to a definition of terrorism that is accepted unanimously by the international community.[5]

A government based on law cannot operate without giving a legal definition of an act it considers unlawful. So, according to a law passed by the U.S. Congress in 1988–1989, the U.S. government defines "terrorism" as "premeditated, politically motivated violence perpetrated against noncombatant targets by subnational groups or clandestine agents."[6] This means that for an act to be considered "terrorism," it must be carried out by a group that is not a government ("subnational"), or by people who are not agents of a government, on citizens or an unarmed civilian population ("non-combatant"). By using this definition, you can see that the 9/11 attacks were clearly "terrorism."

CHAPTER 2

TERRORISM
IN HISTORY

War [on terrorism] would not end until every terrorist group of global reach has been found, stopped, and defeated.
—President George W. Bush in a speech to Congress,
September 20, 2001

If you have been to an airport recently, you must have come face to face with the effects of terrorism. Long lines of people standing patiently, obligingly opening their suitcases for physical inspection, and taking off their shoes before walking through metal detectors testify to how seriously the nation has taken the threats of terrorism. Since we did not have to suffer such indignity to travel in earlier times, you might wonder if terrorism is a recent phenomenon in history.

If by "terrorism" we mean an attempt by a small group to threaten another group of civilians into submission through acts of extreme cruelty, then terrorism has been with us ever since people formed organized societies. However, terrorism consists of much more than acts of violence. Terrorism is the outcome of a specific ideology, an attempt to reshape the world in the ideal image of a specific group. Therefore, in order to understand terrorism, we must focus on the ideas that propel groups of people to kill others and even willingly sacrifice their own lives.

When we turn our attention away from the acts to the ideologies, we see that incidents of terrorism take place in clusters as new ideologies and beliefs arise. And, after some time, the ideas become like a spent force that loses its attraction. A new wave of ideas starts taking its place. In some ways, we can understand the wave effects of terrorism by comparing it to fads and fashions, from bellbottom pants to the length of a skirt. However, terrorism and political violence do not suddenly appear and disappear like fads. They are rooted in definite grievances and injustices perceived by a significant portion of the population.

WAVES OF TERROR

Noted political historian David Rapoport argues that, viewed from a global perspective, acts of terrorism tend to come in clusters, almost like ocean waves. That is why history often seems like a repetitive process. In fact, Rapoport points out that exactly 100 years prior to the 9/11 attacks, in September 1901, William McKinley, the 25th president of the United States, was assassinated by an anarchist. President Theodore Roosevelt, who succeeded McKinley, declared a crusade to exterminate terrorism, much like President George W. Bush did in September 2001. President Roosevelt declared war against terrorism because then, as it is today, the idea of using acts of terrorism to achieve political goals was stirring people all over the world.

By carefully studying the history of the past 125 years, Professor Rapoport identified four waves of global terrorism. The first wave of terrorism was fueled by the "anarchists" in the 1880s and began in Russia. The word *anarchy* comes from the

Greek *anarchos*, which means "having no ruler." The anarchist movement was started by Mikhail Bakunin (1814–1876).

All ideologies are rooted in some real social or political injustice, which the leaders of the movement want to solve by creating a utopian ideal. The leaders claim that these ideal societies existed in the past and can be recreated if only the followers carry out their orders. The indescribable misery of the common Russians at the hands of the powerful inspired the anarchists to kill people of authority in order to create a society in which everybody would be treated equally.[7] The extreme inequality in the European societies of the time made such an ideology extremely attractive, especially to young men

Emma Goldman:
The Disillusioned Anarchist

The lady's floppy hat, stern look, and fiery rhetoric made her an American icon as the nineteenth century was coming to a close. Emma Goldman, born in 1869 in a Jewish ghetto in Russia (in an area that is now Lithuania), was rebellious from childhood. As was the custom, her father tried to marry her off when she was 15, but she refused and was sent to join her sister in Rochester, New York. The young woman soon discovered that her freedom meant slums and sweatshops where she worked as a seamstress. In 1889, the glaring injustices in American society brought Emma to the anarchist movement, which is opposed to all forms of government.

At first, Goldman rejected the entire capitalist system, in which poor workers were exploited without having any rights. She soon realized the need to protect the rights of workers and started to stress the need for personal freedom in her fiery speeches and writings. In 1892, she became involved in a plot with a fellow anarchist, Alexander Berkman, to assassinate Henry Frick, who had brutally suppressed a workers' strike with armed thugs. She even tried to raise money for purchasing a gun by working as a prostitute.

Her speeches in support of the anarchist movement and a woman's right to birth control information attracted the attention and women. Anarchism spread quickly to the Balkans, Western Europe, and, from there, through the newly arriving immigrants to the United States. Anarchism became the first truly international wave of global terrorism.

Europe at the turn of the twentieth century was a virtual tinderbox, with every major power competing for global supremacy. During this period of extreme tension and political rivalry, it was the act of an anarchist that triggered the greatest war the world had ever seen. In 1914, Serbian nationalist Gavrilo Princip assassinated Austrian Archduke Francis Ferdinand and thereby plunged the entire world into World War I.

of the authorities. In 1893, she was sent to prison for urging the unemployed to take bread by force. She was imprisoned a second time in 1916 for distributing birth control literature. She and Berkman were imprisoned for obstructing the military draft during World War I. She was stripped of her U.S. citizenship and, along with some of her fellow revolutionaries, deported to Russia.

However, the repressive Russian society made her completely disillusioned about the communist system. In 1921, she settled in England. If she angered the right with her revolutionary activities in the past, her rejection of the Russian Revolution angered the radical left. Penniless and without friends, Emma was on the verge of being deported from England when a Welsh miner offered to marry her in order to give her British citizenship. She was then able to travel to France and Canada and even allowed to lecture in the United States.

In 1936, Berkman committed suicide, months before the outbreak of the Spanish Civil War. At the age of 67, Goldman went to Spain to join in the struggle. This irrepressible woman, who stood up for equality and social justice, in the end could not believe in any system. Goldman died in 1940.

Anti-colonial movements inspired the second wave of terrorism. The end of World War I produced the 1919 Versailles Peace Treaty, by which the victorious European powers divided the world into colonies. Almost immediately, however, the new wave of terrorism, which was inspired by the ideals of political independence from foreign rule, became active.

After a long and bloody struggle, Britain ended its domination of Ireland but divided the country along religious lines. The Irish provinces with a Catholic majority became an independent nation, the Republic of Ireland, while the northeastern part of the island, where there was a Protestant majority, remained under British rule. The partition of the country saw the rise of the Irish Republican Army (IRA), which aimed to destroy the last vestiges of British colonialism by unifying the island under one (Catholic) rule.

The weakening of the victorious powers after World War II gave new strength to the anti-colonial movements in the 1940s and 1950s. In Palestine, the Stern and Irgun gangs, Jewish terrorist groups dedicated to the ideals of creating an independent state of Israel, started a campaign of attacks against the British and the Arabs. In the mid 1950s, the Greek nationalist group EOKA (Ethniki Organosis Kyprion Agoniston) led a successful campaign of violence against the British and Turkish authorities. Terrorist groups sprung up all over the colonies, from Southeast Asia to North Africa. The second wave of terrorism ended when the European empires broke up after World War II and the former colonies gained independence. But, as the second wave of international terrorism ended, the third wave of terrorism was beginning to gather momentum.

Advancements in science and technology brought the world closer together. As we learned more about each other, it became possible not only to communicate with people from distant lands but also to allow revolutionary ideals to spread quickly around the globe.

After World War I, anarchism as an ideological force declined in strength throughout the world. However, old ideas do not get totally discredited or destroyed unless the social and economic conditions that created them are altered significantly. The persistent problems of poverty and social injustice, which spawned anarchism in the late 1800s, transformed into the third wave of transnational Marxist and other left-wing terrorism in the 1960s and 1970s. Marxist movements were rooted in the writings of German philosopher Karl Marx (1818–1883), who claimed that in a capitalist society, those who own the capital always exploit the working class. Thus, the only way the working class could become free of exploitation would be through violent revolution. All the communist countries in the world were based on the principles of Marxism.

The defining moment for the third wave of terrorism came with the Vietnam War. The daily sight of violence on television screens revitalized the leftist movement. The fact that an ill-equipped, ragtag band of Viet Cong guerrillas could defeat the U.S. Armed Forces caught the imagination of many around the world. The Weather Underground in the United States, the Red Army Faction in West Germany and Japan, the Red Brigade in Italy, and *Action Directe* in France started planting bombs and staged shooting attacks.

In Northern Ireland, the IRA was able to transform its religion-based movement into a part of the global leftist movement, which renewed the strength of the organization. A similar transformation reinvigorated the Basque separatist group, ETA, in Spain. In the Middle East, the secular and left-leaning Palestine Liberation Organization (PLO) and its affiliates, such as the Popular Front for the Liberation of Israel (PFLP), began a campaign of terror by hijacking airplanes. In Latin America, the popularity of Marxist ideologues and strategists such as Che Guevara and Carlos Marighela proved irresistible to many youthful followers. Che even became a cultural icon for the time. The Tupamaros guerrilla groups in Uruguay and

Eric Robert Rudoph:
The Terrorist Next Door

Terrorists come in many different guises. They can be from any religion, nationality, and ethnicity, or they may not be affiliated with any group. Eric Robert Rudolph is a prime example of how diverse terrorists can be. Born in 1966, Rudolph was a good-looking, charismatic young man, who was an avid survivalist and obsessed with "Christian Identity" ideology. This ideology mixes Christian fundamentalist beliefs with racism and extremes of patriotism. The foundation of this ideology is the belief that white Americans are God's chosen people. In order to establish God's kingdom on Earth, they are at war with homosexuality, abortion, prostitution, and anybody who is not Christian and white.

Rudolph found a ready community of like-minded people in the southeastern part of the United States and, without being part of any one organization, mingled with various white supremacist groups. With time, Rudolph took up arms against those he considered enemies. On July 27, 1996, during the Atlanta Olympics, Rudolph planted a bomb that killed an innocent woman and injured more than 100 other people. His targeting of the Olympics was perhaps due to the event's celebration of multiculturalism or his perception of it as a manifestation of a new world order, where the United States is stripped of its dominant position.

The following year, Rudolph bombed a lesbian nightclub in Georgia and, in 1998, he planted a bomb outside an abortion clinic, killing an off-duty police officer and seriously wounding another person. By this time, the police had identified Rudolph as the attacker and he was on the FBI's Ten Most Wanted list.

Rudolph headed for the hills in rural North Carolina. His survivalist training paid off and, with the help of people who sympathized with his political views, he evaded capture for nearly five years. Finally, he was arrested while rummaging though a dumpster in Murphy, North Carolina, on May 31, 2003. Rudolph was brought to trial and faced the death sentence. However, he made a plea agreement with the prosecution and, as a result, is currently serving four consecutive life sentences without the possibility of parole.

Argentina, the Shining Path in Peru, and the FARC in Colombia became active at this time. In India, inspired by the communist ideology promoted by China's Mao Ze-dong, the Naxalite movement started its urban guerrilla attacks.

Once again, as with the other waves in the past, this wave of global terrorism saw its decline. In the 1980s, many of the third-wave groups had suffered military defeats at the hands of the security and armed forces of the countries in which they were operating. The lack of popular support dealt a devastating blow to the radical groups in Europe and the United States.

Finally, in the 1990s, the stalwarts of communism faltered: The Soviet Union collapsed from within and Revolutionary China became a bastion of hyper-capitalism. Being robbed of the champions of left-wing radicalism, many of these terrorist groups found it impossible to carry on. However, as I mentioned before, old ideas do not totally disappear unless the conditions that gave rise to such ideas go through radical changes—today, the leftist ideology is staging a comeback in parts of India and in the neighboring mountain nation of Nepal.

Professor Rapoport argues that we are currently in the fourth wave of global terrorism, which started in the early 1990s. This wave is fueled not by Marxism or even nationalism—the primary driving force of this wave of terrorism is religious fundamentalism. The ethnic and national identity of a minority group within a large country often coincides with religious differences. For example, the Catholic minority in Northern Ireland, the Hindu minority in Buddhist Sri Lanka, or the Sikh minority in Hindu India are cases where religion and nationalist aspirations are closely intertwined. However, the central force of the fourth wave is different; today's funda-mentalist movements aim not only at replacing the current governments but also at transforming their nations into the group's own image of religious purity.

Few countries in the world are free of these kinds of religious extremist movements. In the United States, the "Christian

The Sikh soldiers shown here are members of India's security forces. By contrast, in 1985, a Sikh extremist group in India planted a bomb and brought down an Air India airliner, killing nearly 200 people.

Identity" movement inspired a number of loosely formed groups or clusters of individuals. In 1985, a Sikh extremist group in India planted a bomb and brought down an Air India 747 in midair, killing nearly 200 passengers and crew members. In 1994, a Jewish physician, part of a radical terrorist group, murdered 29 Arab worshipers in the tomb of Abraham, located in the city of Hebron. The 1995 Oklahoma City bombing was carried out by people who were at least ideologically associated with the Christian Identity movement.[8] In the same year, the Japanese religious sect Aum Shinrikyo released the deadly nerve gas sarin in the Tokyo subway, killing 12 and injuring over 3,000 people.

However, in terms of destructive capabilities, none of these religious groups can come close to the Islamic groups operating in many parts of the Arab/Islamic world. No group in history has been able to kill so many as did al Qaeda in the attacks of 9/11. Similarly, no other groups can match the ability of Hamas, the Palestine Islamic Jihad, and other groups in continuing a sustained attack of lethal suicide bombing in Israel. We will discuss the causes of Islamic terrorism later in the book.

The concept of waves of terrorism points to a number of important conclusions. It shows how ideas can move across continents and affect people at a certain time in history. Unfortunately, as one wave wanes, another one generally picks up steam. Therefore, it seems that the war against terrorism cannot be won. Yet it also shows that, although the world may never be free of destructive acts carried out by disgruntled groups, the ideas that spawn terrorism have a definite life span. History cannot predict how long the current wave of religious fundamentalism will provide fuel for the fires of violence. But, if the past is any indicator, we can at least find comfort in the thought that some time, in the not too distant future, this wave will also run its course.

CHAPTER 3

TERRORIST GROUPS

These days, as our airwaves are filled with the news of our confrontation with terrorism coming out of the Islamic world, it is easy to equate the two. Yet, terrorism can come from nearly every corner of the world and from people of every religion. Each year, the U.S. State Department publishes a list of terrorist groups.[9] You should note, however, that this list includes only those groups that the State Department considers to be terrorists and that pose the biggest threat to the United States' interests.

Besides these groups, there are many others from all around the world that pose a clear and present danger but do not show up on our radar. For example, there is a Maoist group in Nepal called the Communist Party of Nepal (Maoist), or CP-M, that is fighting to replace the current government with a communist regime. Nepal, being an impoverished and remote Himalayan country, does not register on the global stage. Therefore, the CP-M did not make the State Department's list in 2004. However, it could very well show up in subsequent years' lists of terrorist groups.

There is another problem with making a list of terrorist groups. These groups, being secretive organizations, often change their names and a single group may be known by several names. Adding to the confusion, a group may not want to claim responsibility for its actions after staging an attack. So, the authorities may not know which group carried out the attack or the group may invent a fictitious name in which it will claim responsibility. Also, several groups may cooperate in a joint action. For example, on several occasions, Hamas and Palestinian Islamic Jihad have coordinated their efforts in staging an attack. These are some of the problems inherent in terrorism research.

Below is a list of the most prominent groups that the U.S. State Department considered "terrorists" in 2004, along with a brief description of each group. This list of the various terrorist groups will not only introduce you to the problem of terrorism around the world, but will also show you how many of these groups are interconnected. However, you should know that the descriptions are only superficial, since the story of each group is embedded in the culture, history, and politics of its region.

If you are interested in learning more about these groups, you can conduct your own research. You can learn a lot about a group by simply searching the Internet for its name. There are also some resources, such as the Naval Postgraduate School Website (http://www.nps.edu/Library), that can give you more detailed information. There are also numerous books and articles on these terrorist groups.

ABU NIDAL ORGANIZATION (ANO)

The Abu Nidal Organization (ANO) is known by the *nom de*

guerre of its leader, Sabri al-Banna, who took the name Abu Nidal.[10] The ANO's goal is to establish a free Palestinian state. It is responsible for attacks in 20 countries that have killed and wounded nearly 900 people from Israel, the United States, Great Britain, France, and pro-Western Arab countries. It has even assassinated high level officials of the Palestine Liberation Organization (PLO), whom it considered to be "soft" on Israel. The group was highly active in the 1970s and 1980s, but has not staged any major attacks since 1994. After the death of its leader, Abu Nidal, in 2002 in Baghdad, the group's strength is not known.

ABU SAYYAF GROUP (ASG)

Abu Sayyaf Group (ASG) is a relatively small Muslim group active in the Philippines. The ASG claims to fight for a separate Islamic state in the southern archipelago in the Sulu Sea off the eastern coast of Malaysia. Some of its leadership has ties to al Qaeda. However, it is far more interested in making money from kidnapping and hostage-taking than in Islamic jihad. Because of the criminal nature of the group, Osama bin Laden and al Qaeda cut off their relationships with the ASG. For similar reasons, it also split from the Midanao-based separatist Islamic group in the Philippines called the Moro Liberation Front.

AL-AQSA MARTYRS BRIGADE

The Al-Aqsa Martyrs Brigade is named after the famous Al-Aqsa Mosque in Jerusalem. After secret negotiations held in Oslo, Norway, on September 13, 1993, the main Palestinian group, the Palestine Liberation Organization (PLO), signed an agreement with the Israeli government for a negotiated settlement of their conflict. However, the process ended in a stalemate in December 2000. The failure of the peace process saw the establishment of this radical group affiliated with the PLO. Its immediate aim includes driving out the Israeli Army and the Jewish settlers from the West Bank and the Gaza Strip and

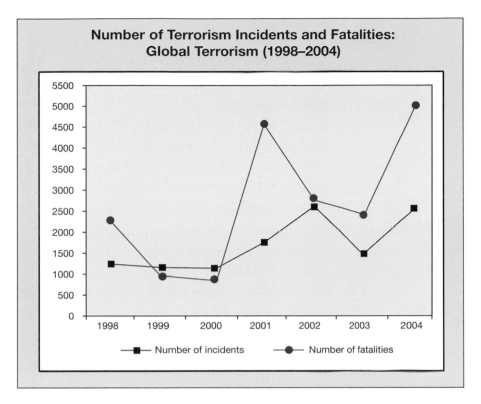

Number of Terrorism Incidents and Fatalities:
Global Terrorism (1998–2004)

■ Number of incidents   ● Number of fatalities

Table 3.1 This graph shows the number of incidents and fatalities from terrorism worldwide. As you can see, the trend was going down when the attacks of 2001 changed it radically. The war in Iraq and the consequent insurgency made a huge difference in the frequency of incidents and the number of fatalities from terrorist attacks.

establishing a Palestinian state. This violent group specializes in shootings and suicide attacks.

ANSAR AL-ISLAM

Ansar al-Islam is a radical Islamic group that intends to establish strict Islamic rule through violent jihad. Its name means "the supporters of Islam." It was operating in northern Iraq on the Iranian border when the U.S.-led invasion started in 2003. The U.S. claims that the group has ties with al Qaeda and that it has attempted to produce deadly chemical weapons. Ansar al-Islam has staged a number of spectacular suicide attacks in Iraq, targeting U.S. forces along with the group's Kurdish rivals, and killing and injuring a large number of people.

ARMED ISLAMIC GROUP (GIA)

The Armed Islamic Group (GIA) is located in the North African country of Algeria and aims at overthrowing its secular government. The group was formed in 1992 when Algeria was scheduled to have an election. Because the radical Islamic party Islamic Salvation Front was certain to win, Algeria's largely secular military staged a successful coup in 1992. The GIA aims at overthrowing the current government and replacing it with a strict Islamic state. The GIA has been involved in widespread massacres of civilians, including expatriate Europeans, and also engages in car bombings, assassinations, and hostage-taking. They do not have any known connection to the global jihadi movement.

ASBAT AL-ANSAR

Asbat al-Ansar is a radical Sunni Muslim group located in Lebanon. Its members are primarily exiled Palestinians. They are linked with al Qaeda and believe in an extreme interpretation of Islam. The group aims at overthrowing the current Lebanese government and transforming the country into a strict Islamic model. They have used car bombs and attacks on rival groups.

AUM SHINRIKYO

Aum Shinrikyo is a Japanese religious cult group that draws heavily from Hindu and Buddhist images and teachings. It was established in 1987 by Shoko Asahara (born Chizuo Matsumoto), with the goal of taking over Japan and then the rest of world to form a global society after its own image. Its most spectacular attack took place on March 20, 1995, when Aum members brought six packages and poked them with umbrella

Shoko Asahara, shown here, is the founder of the Aum Shinrikyo cult. This group is best known for releasing deadly sarin gas in the Tokyo subway system in 1995, killing 12 people and injuring nearly 5,000 others.

tips to release deadly sarin gas in the crowded Tokyo subway. The attack killed 12 and injured nearly 5,000 commuters. Although Asahara was arrested and is now in prison, a number of top leaders of Aum Shinrikyo are still at large. Besides Japan, the group is said to have a following in Australia, Russia, Ukraine, Sri Lanka, the former Yugoslavia, and the United States.

BASQUE FATHERLAND AND LIBERTY (ETA)

Basque Fatherland and Liberty (ETA) is a leftist group that uses terrorism to fight for the formation of an independent Basque state in parts of northern Spain and southwest France. The group is known by its acronym, ETA, which stands for *Euskadi ta Askatasuna* ("Basque Fatherland and Liberty" in the Basque language). Basques are a unique group, culturally and linguistically different from the Spaniards and the French. ETA targets mostly government buildings and symbols of Spanish authority by using remote-controlled bombs. They have also engaged in high-profile assassinations of government officials and politicians as well as journalists and other civic leaders, particularly in the Basque region.

COMMUNIST PARTY OF THE PHILIPPINES/NEW PEOPLE'S ARMY (CPP/NPA)

Communist Party of the Philippines/New People's Army (CPP/NPA) is a guerrilla group that operates in the rural areas of the Philippines. The group's goal is to replace the current government and establish a communist system. It opposes any U.S. presence in the island nation and has targeted U.S. service personnel as well as embassy personnel stationed in the Philippines.

GAMA'A AL-ISLAMIYYA (ISLAMIC GROUP OR IG)

Gama'a al-Islamiyya (Islamic Group or IG) is the largest radical Islamic group in Egypt. They have been active since the late 1970s and aim at transforming the secular society of Egypt into a strict Islamic one. The IG's most notable activity was its involvement in the 1993 bombing of the World Trade Center. The group's blind spiritual leader, Shaykh Umar Abd al-Rahman, was arrested for the attack and is currently serving time in a U.S. prison. Although the group has split into several factions, its members are still active in Egypt and in many other parts of the world.

HAMAS (ISLAMIC RESISTANCE MOVEMENT)

Hamas ranks among the most deadly terrorist organizations in the world. The word *Hamas*, which means "courage" or "bravery" in Arabic, is an acronym for *Harakat al-Muqawamah al-Islamiyya* (Islamic Resistance Movement). It is a fundamentalist, Sunni Islamic organization, which aims at the destruction of Israel and the creation of a fundamentalist society in Palestine. The group started as a charitable organization providing basic health care and Islamic education to poor Palestinians in the West Bank and Gaza Strip. It became involved in the street violence called *intifada* ("uprising"), where the Palestinian youth started attacking Israeli military forces and civilians by throwing rocks. When the Palestine Liberation Organization (PLO) signed the Oslo Agreement with the government of Israel in 1993, Hamas, being opposed to any compromise with the Jewish state, started its violent campaign of suicide attacks and car bombings aimed at Israeli civilians and members of the armed forces. Over the years, many of its leaders have been killed or put in prison by the Israeli government, yet it still commands strong support among Palestinians and remains a potent force in the Middle East conflict.

HARAKAT UL-MUJAHIDIN (HUM)

Harakat ul-Mujahidin (HUM) is an Islamic militant group based in Pakistan that operates primarily in the disputed territory of Kashmir. In 1947, when British colonial rule ended, two countries, India and Pakistan, were created. The former princely state of Kashmir was claimed by both countries. A year later, the first war between the two countries broke out

al-Zawahiri, the second-in-command to Osama bin Laden, were members of the EIJ. In 1998, under the intellectual leadership of al-Zawahiri, an alliance between the two groups was formed as a grand alliance of "International Front for Jihad against Jews and Crusaders." The EIJ's activities came to the attention of the world in 1981 when it assassinated Egyptian President Anwar Sadat for cooperating with Israel. Its members fanned out across the world and took part in attacking many Western targets, including the 9/11 hijackings.

KAHANE CHAI (KACH)

Kahane Chai (Kach) was founded by a radical American Jewish rabbi named Meir Kahane. The original name of his movement was *Kach*, a Hebrew word meaning "only thus." The stated goal of Kach is to restore the Biblical state of Israel. On November 5, 1990, Meir Kahane was murdered in New York by an Islamic fanatic from Egypt. Meir's son, Binyamin, took over the movement and named it Kahane Chai, which means "Kahane Lives." In February 1994, another American-born Jewish radical, Dr. Baruch Goldstein, opened fire on Muslims praying in the Cave of the Patriarchs in Hebron (which is holy to both Jews and Muslims), killing 29. The Kahane Chai issued a statement of support for the acts of Goldstein. This and other acts caused both the U.S. and Israeli governments to declare Kahane Chai a terrorist organization.

KURDISTAN WORKERS' PARTY (PKK)

The Kurdistan Workers' Party (PKK) is a Marxist-Leninist insurgent group, also known as Kurdistan Freedom and Democracy Congress (KADEK). Kurds are a non-Arab minority population in the Middle East with a distinct language and culture. The bulk of the Kurdish population lives in eastern Turkey, northeastern Iraq, and northwestern Iran. A smaller number of Kurds also live in northeast Syria and southern Armenia.

The radical Jewish group Kahane Chai was founded by an American rabbi named Meir Kahane, pictured above. Kahane Chai's stated goal is to restore the Biblical state of Israel. Meir Kahane was murdered by an Islamic fanatic in 1990, but his son took leadership of the group.

The PKK was founded in 1978 and is primarily composed of Turkish Kurds. The group's goal is to establish an independent, democratic Kurdish state in the Middle East. In the early 1990s, the PKK moved beyond rural-based insurgent activities to include urban terrorism. The PKK conducted attacks on Turkish diplomatic and commercial facilities in dozens of West European cities in 1993 and again in the spring of 1995. Also around that time, the PKK targeted Turkey's tourist industry, bombing tourist sites and hotels and kidnapping several foreign tourists. In early 1999, Turkish authorities captured the charismatic leader of the group, Abdullah Ocalan. Although he remains in the prison, Ocalan declared a ceasefire and promised to work within the Turkish democratic system.

LASHKAR-E TAYYIBA (LT OR ARMY OF THE RIGHTEOUS)

Lashkar-e Tayyiba (LT or Army of the Righteous) is a Sunni Muslim organization based in Pakistan. Formed in 1989, it is one of the best trained separatist groups fighting the Indian authorities in Kashmir. It is also extremely religious in its orientation and is virulently anti-American. On numerous occasions, the LT has engaged Indian troops and targeted the civilian population in Indian-held Kashmir. The Indian government implicated the LT along with Jaish-e-Mohammed in the 2001 attack on the Indian Parliament. In March 2002, a coordinated operation by the Pakistani authorities and U.S. intelligence nabbed Abu Zubaydah, a senior al Qaeda official, in a safe house operated by the LT, suggesting a close link between the two groups.

LASHKAR I JHANGVI (LJ)

Lashkar i Jhangvi (LJ) is a particularly violent terrorist organization based in Pakistan. LJ is Sunni Muslim group whose original targets included Shiite Muslims and their Iranian supporters (Iran is a predominantly Shiite country). However, over time, it became a jihadi group, which started making high-profile attacks on Westerners in Pakistan. It was primarily responsible for the 2002 kidnapping and murder of *Wall Street Journal* reporter Daniel Pearl. LJ's link to al Qaeda is well documented.

LIBERATION TIGERS OF TAMIL EELAM (LTTE)

The Liberation Tigers of Tamil Eelam (LTTE) was founded in 1976 with the aim of creating a separate Tamil nation in the northern part of the island of Sri Lanka, where the majority Sinhalese government is locked in a civil war with the Tamil minority. The Sinhalese are Buddhist, while the Tamils are primarily Hindus. The LTTE started an armed conflict in 1983 and has used its elite Black Tiger squad to conduct a long and bloody campaign of suicide bombing. In fact, nearly a decade before the various Palestinian groups and al Qaeda brought

The Liberation Tigers of Tamil fight for a separate Tamil nation in the northern part of the island of Sri Lanka. Their current leader, Velupillai Prabhakaran, is show above addressing the Tamils.

them to prominence, the LTTE nearly perfected the devastating tactics of suicide attacks. Apart from claiming the lives of many Sri Lankans, in its most high-profile assassination, the LTTE killed former Indian Prime Minister Rajiv Gandhi in 1991. The LTTE has a highly structured organization under the leadership of Velupillai Prabhakaran, with its own finance department, intelligence services, and even a small naval unit called the Sea Tigers.

MUJAHEDIN-E KHALQ ORGANIZATION (MEK)

Mujahedin-e Khalq Organization (MEK) is an Iranian-based terrorist organization that mixes the atheistic but egalitarian principles of Marxism with a radical interpretation of Islam. The MEK came into prominence through its anti-Western attacks in Iran and abroad. However, recently, the MEK has started fighting to overthrow the Iranian clerics and form their own government.

NATIONAL LIBERATION ARMY (ELN)

The National Liberation Army (ELN) is a Colombian Marxist group formed in 1965 by a group of urban intellectuals following in the path of Fidel Castro and Che Guevara. The ELN engages in kidnapping, extortion, hijacking, and bombing. Their goals involve transforming Colombia into a Cuba-type communist state. The group often targets foreign workers in the country's petrochemical industry for ransom. It is also involved in drug trafficking.

PALESTINIAN ISLAMIC JIHAD (PIJ)

Palestinian Islamic Jihad (PIJ) is a militant group located in the Gaza Strip. Like all other jihadi groups, it wants to establish a strict Islamic state, first in Palestine by destroying Israel, and then in the rest of the Arab/Islamic world. Hence, it also targets other pro-Western moderate Arab regimes. Since the late 1980s, along with Hamas and other radical Palestinian groups, the PIJ has carried out a relentless campaign of suicide attacks against Israeli civilian and military populations.

PALESTINE LIBERATION FRONT (PLF)

The Palestine Liberation Front (PLF) is a Lebanon-based Palestinian organization. It was formed as part of a split from the Popular Front for the Liberation of Palestine (PFLP). Both the PLF and the PFLP are inspired by Marxist ideology and claim to speak for the poorest of the Palestinian community. The PLF attacks Israel across its northern border from Lebanon. This group is part of the largest Palestinian organization, the Palestine Liberation Organization (PLO), founded by Yasir Arafat.

POPULAR FRONT FOR THE LIBERATION OF PALESTINE (PFLP)

The Popular Front for the Liberation of Palestine (PFLP) was established in 1967 by George Habash. The PFLP was one of the original coalition of groups that started the Palestinian umbrella organization, the PLO. However, in 1993, a rift developed over PLO chairman Yasir Arafat's decision to work with Israel for a peaceful settlement of the conflict, since the PFLP did not want to recognize the right of Israel to exist. The PFLP undertook a relatively small number of suicide bombings in Isreal and also carried out a number of car bombings.

PFLP-GENERAL COMMAND (PFLP-GC)

About a year after the formation of the PFLP, a number of its more radical members accused their leader, George Habash, of being too interested in politics and not committed to fighting Israel. They formed the PFLP-General Command (PFLP-GC). This group has carried out a number of violent attacks in Europe and in a number of countries in the Middle East. It also operates in southern Lebanon and in Israel.

AL QAEDA

Today, the best known terrorist group is al Qaeda, headed by Osama bin Laden. In Arabic, the term *al Qaeda* means "the base." In the mid-1980s, bin Laden and others founded the group to serve as a base for the Arab mujahideen fighting the Soviet military in Afghanistan.

A U.S. soldier fighting overseas can keep in touch with family members through the services of the U.S. military. However, when the young men from Arab countries went to Afghanistan to join the jihad against the Soviet Union, they were not part of any organized military. Therefore, there was no supply line linking them to their families back home. Al Qaeda filled this need by becoming a base for the mujahideen fighters.

Soon, Ayman al-Zawahiri of Egyptian Islamic Jihad joined al Qaeda in Afghanistan. Osama bin Laden had a lot of his own money and, being from one of the wealthiest families of Saudi Arabia, he was extremely well connected, which allowed him to raise even more money. To this, al-Zawahiri and his experienced band of Egyptian rebels contributed ideological zeal and organizational capabilities. Together, al Qaeda soon emerged as a formidable force.

In the beginning, al Qaeda fought Soviet forces in Afghanistan alongside the United States and its allies, Pakistan and Saudi Arabia. After the defeat of the Soviet Union, al Qaeda was interested in establishing Islamic fundamentalist societies in Egypt and Yemen. However, in 1990–1991, when the U.S.-led forces fought the Gulf War against Iraq, bin Laden and his followers became concerned. To them, it appeared that the war was an American ploy to control Arab oil reserves. Also, to the Islamic fundamentalists, establishing U.S. military bases inside Saudi Arabia, the birthplace of the prophet Muhammed, was considered sacrilegious. Inevitably, al Qaeda declared its holy war against the United States.

REAL IRA (RIRA)

One of the world's longest running sectarian wars centers around the question of Northern Ireland. The dispute has roots in the conflict between the indigenous Gaelic people and the invading Anglo-Normans in 1169, which made Ireland a British colony. The conflict deepened when King Henry VIII force-fully imposed Protestantism on the Irish Catholics. The fight for Irish independence from British rule also took the form of a religious and cultural struggle.[11]

In 1921, Ireland gained independence, but the northern part of Ireland, where the Protestants are a majority (60%), remained part of the United Kingdom. At this time, the Irish Republican Army (IRA) was created to forcefully unite North-ern Ireland with the Republic of Ireland, where Catholics make up nearly 97% of the population. After nearly 60 years of sectarian bloodshed, by signing the Good Friday Accord on

April 10, 1998, the mainstream members of the IRA came to accept a political reconciliation with their Protestant rivals. But, a group of disgruntled radicals formed a group to continue the fight, called the "Real" IRA (RIRA). Since then, the RIRA has engaged in numerous bombings, assassinations, and robberies, the most notorious of which was a 1998 bombing in the busy shopping area of Omagh, where 28 people were killed.

REVOLUTIONARY ARMED FORCES OF COLOMBIA (FARC)

Revolutionary Armed Forces of Colombia (FARC) is a guerrilla force inspired by communist ideology. It traces its origin to the troubled days of Colombian history in the 1950s when the militias of the "conservative" wealthy landlords were fighting with the leftist "liberal" militias. FARC was formally established in 1964. Today, this group controls large parts of the Colombian countryside and is engaged in large-scale drug trafficking. Its activities include car bombings and hostage taking for large ransoms.

REVOLUTIONARY NUCLEI (RN)

Revolutionary Nuclei (RN) is a leftist group that operates out of Greece. In its ideology, the RN is against Western-style capitalism and violently opposes the military alliance between the United States and the North Atlantic Treaty Organization (NATO), of which Greece is a member. The RN typically bombs buildings and business establishments and sends warning calls shortly before the explosion to minimize the loss of human lives. It has bombed a number of establishments in Athens and other parts of Greece.

REVOLUTIONARY ORGANIZATION 17 NOVEMBER (RO)

On November 17, 1973, when Greece was ruled by a group of military generals, a student uprising was crushed by the use of brute force by the Greek dictator. The killings of the students gave birth to the radical leftist Revolutionary Organization

17 November (RO). The group has a similar ideological orientation and mode of operation to the Revolutionary Nuclei.

REVOLUTIONARY PEOPLE'S LIBERATION ARMY/FRONT (DHKP/C)

The Revolutionary People's Liberation Army/Front (DHKP/C) is a radical Marxist group based in Turkey and is virulently anti-American. It was originally established as Devrimci Sol and was renamed in 1994. Since the late 1980s, it has staged many attacks against U.S. interests and symbols, including a rocket attack on the American embassy in Istanbul in 1992, protesting U.S. involvement in the Gulf War.

SALAFIST GROUP FOR CALL AND COMBAT (GSPC)

Salafist Group for Call and Combat (GSPC) came out of the violent Armed Islamic Group (GIA) in Algeria. When the GIA started to slaughter large numbers of innocent civilians, it lost a lot of popular support. However, there were many in Algeria who were still sympathetic to the idea of getting rid of the military dictatorship and replacing it with an Islamic regime. The GSPC represents these ideals and, instead of targeting civilians, they attack military and government officials. Some believe that GSPC maintains a link with al Qaeda.

SHINING PATH (SENDERO LUMINOSO OR SL)

Extreme inequalities in Peruvian society gave rise to the Marxist group Shining Path (Sendero Luminoso or SL), founded by a former university professor, Abimael Guzman. In the 1980s, this group nearly paralyzed the entire country of Peru with its assassinations, bombings, kidnappings, and hostage taking. In the 1990s, government forces became more successful in suppressing the SL by capturing many of its top leaders. However, recent reports suggest that it may be once again regrouping by generating funds through drug trafficking and hostage taking.

UNITED SELF-DEFENSE FORCES OF COLOMBIA (AUC)

United Self-Defense Forces of Colombia (AUC) is a paramilitary force representing rich landlords, right-wing drug traffickers, and other pro-government interest groups fighting the Marxist guerrilla groups in Colombia. It often attacks politicians and others in Colombian society sympathetic to the leftist cause. It has also attacked and slaughtered entire villages in order to control drug trafficking.

CHAPTER 4

TERRORIST LEADERS OR PEACEMAKERS?

Can anyone blame you if you think of Osama bin Laden as the poster child for the evils of terrorism? His menacing words, which show no sign of remorse for killing so many innocent people all over the world, are aimed directly for our hearts. Looking at photographs of him, it is almost impossible to imagine that someday he could be considered a hero by people all over the world, including in the United States, the primary target of his wrath.

Strange as it may sound, history is full of examples where those who have been considered "terrorists" under different circumstances have been able to command wide-ranging respect even from those who were in their cross-hairs. In this chapter, I will give you examples of three individuals who were considered "terrorists" at one point in their lives, but later were praised as peacemakers, and even given the highest honor in the area of world peace: the Nobel Peace Prize. Here arc their stories, as told by the Nobel Prize Committee:

YASIR ARAFAT

Mohammed Abdel-Raouf Arafat As Qudwa al-Hussaeini was born on 24 August 1929 in Cairo,[12] his father a textile merchant who was a Palestinian with some Egyptian ancestry, his mother from an old Palestinian family in Jerusalem. She died when Yasir, as he was called, was five years old, and he was sent to live with his maternal uncle in Jerusalem, the capital of Palestine, then under British rule, which the Palestinians were opposing. He has revealed little about his childhood, but one of his earliest memories is of British soldiers breaking into his uncle's house after midnight, beating members of the family and smashing furniture.

After four years in Jerusalem, his father brought him back to Cairo, where an older sister took care of him and his siblings. Arafat never mentions his father, who was not close to his children. Arafat did not attend his father's funeral in 1952.

In Cairo, before he was seventeen Arafat was smuggling arms to Palestine to be used against the British and the Jews. At nineteen, during the war between the Jews and the Arab states, Arafat left his studies at the University of Faud I (later Cairo University) to fight against the Jews in the Gaza area. The defeat of the Arabs and the establishment of the state of Israel left him in such despair that he applied for a visa to study at the University of Texas. Recovering his spirits and retaining his dream of an independent Palestinian homeland, he returned to Faud University to major in engineering but spent most of his time as leader of the Palestinian students.

He did manage to get his degree in 1956, worked briefly in Egypt, then resettled in Kuwait, first being employed in the

Yasir Arafat, shown here, was the chairman of the Palestinian Liberation Organization's executive committee until his death in 2004. Arafat was awarded the Nobel Peace Prize in 1994 for his efforts to make peace between Israel and Palestine. The prize was also awarded to Prime Minister Yitzhak Rabin and Foreign Minister Shimon Peres of Israel.

department of public works, next successfully running his own contracting firm. He spent all his spare time in political activities, to which he contributed most of the profits. In 1958 he and his friends founded Al-Fatah, an underground network of secret cells, which in 1959 began to publish a magazine advocating armed struggle against Israel. At the end of 1964 Arafat left Kuwait to become a full-time revolutionary, organising Fatah raids into Israel from Jordan.

It was also in 1964 that the Palestine Liberation Organisation (PLO) was established, under the sponsorship of the Arab League, bringing together a number of groups all working to free Palestine for the Palestinians. The Arab states favoured a more conciliatory policy than Fatah's, but after their defeat by Israel in the 1967 Six-Day War, Fatah emerged from the underground as the most powerful and best organised of the groups making up the PLO, took over that organisation in 1969 when Arafat became the chairman of the PLO executive committee. The PLO was no longer to be something of a puppet organisation of the Arab states, wanting to keep the Palestinians quiet, but an independent nationalist organisation, based in Jordan.

Arafat developed the PLO into a state within the state of Jordan with its own military forces. King Hussein of Jordan, disturbed by its guerrilla attacks on Israel and other violent methods, eventually expelled the PLO from his country. Arafat sought to build a similar organisation in Lebanon, but this time was driven out by an Israeli military invasion. He kept the organization alive, however, by moving its headquarters to Tunis. He was a survivor himself, escaping death in an airplane crash, surviving any assassination attempts by Israeli intelligence agencies, and recovering from a serious stroke.

His life was one of constant travel, moving from country to country to promote the Palestinian cause, always keeping his movements secret, as he did any details about his private life. Even his marriage to Suha Tawil, a Palestinian half his age, was kept secret for some fifteen months. She had already begun significant humanitarian activities at home, especially for disabled children, but the prominent part she took in the public events in Oslo was a surprise for many Arafat-watchers. Since then, their daughter, Zahwa, named after Arafat's mother, has been born.

The period after the expulsion from Lebanon was a low time for Arafat and the PLO. Then the *intifada* (shaking) protest movement strengthened Arafat by directing world attention to the difficult plight of the Palestinians. In 1988 came a change of policy. In a speech at a special United Nations session held in Geneva, Switzerland, Arafat declared that the PLO renounced terrorism and supported "the right of all parties concerned in the Middle East conflict to live in peace and security, including the state of Palestine, Israel and other neighbors".

The prospects for a peace agreement with Israel now brightened. After a setback when the PLO supported Iraq in the Persian Gulf War of 1991, the peace process began in earnest, leading to the Oslo Accords of 1993.

This agreement included provision for the Palestinian

elections which took place in early 1996, and Arafat was elected President of the Palestine Authority. Like other Arab regimes in the area, however, Arafat's governing style tended to be more dictatorial than democratic. When the right-wing government of Benjamin Netanyahu came to power in Israel in 1996, the peace process slowed down considerably. Much depends upon the nature of the new Israeli government, which will result from the elections to be held in 1999.

Note: Yasir Arafat died on November 11, 2004.
Source: From *Nobel Lectures, Peace 1991–1995*, Editor Irwin Abrams, World Scientific Publishing Co., Singapore, 1999. Copyright © 1994 The Nobel Foundation. Reprinted by permission.

MENACHEM BEGIN

Menachem Begin was born in Brest-Litovsk, Poland on 16 August 1913, son of Zeev-Dov and Hassia Begin. He was educated at the Mizrachi Hebrew School and the Polish Gymnasium (High School). In 1931, he entered Warsaw University and took his law degree in 1935.

Until the age of 13 he belonged to the Hashomer Hatza'ir scout movement, and at the age of 16 joined Betar (Brit Trumpeldor), the nationalist youth movement associated with the Zionist Revisionist Movement. In 1932 he became head of the Organization Department of Betar for Poland travelling on its behalf throughout the country, and contributing many articles to the revisionist press. He was sent to Czechoslovakia to head the movement there.

In 1937 he returned to Poland, and for a time was imprisoned for leading a demonstration, in front of the British Legation in Warsaw, protesting against British policy in Palestine. He organized groups of Betar members who went to Palestine as illegal immigrants, and in 1939 became the head of the movement in Poland. On the outbreak of World War II, he was arrested by the Russian authorities and in 1940-41 was confined

**Menachem Begin, former
Jewish underground leader,
is shown here at a news
conference in London on
January 10, 1972. Begin
served as prime minister
of Israel from 1977 to 1983.**

in concentration camps in Siberia and elsewhere, but was
released under the terms of the Stalin-Sikorski agreement.

On his release he joined the Polish army and was trans-
ferred to the Middle East. After demobilization, in 1943, he
assumed command of the Irgun Zvati Leumi (National Military
Organization), known by the initials of its Hebrew name as
"Etzel". In this capacity he directed Etzel's operations against
the British, and the Palestine Government offered a reward of
£ 10,000 for information leading to his arrest, but he evaded
capture by living in disguise in Tel Aviv. In 1947, he met in
secret with several members of the United Nations Special
Committee on Palestine as well as the foreign press, to explain
the outlook of his movement.

After the establishment of the State of Israel, he founded
the Herut Movement, together with his colleagues, and headed
the party's list of candidates for the Knesset. He has been a
member of the Knesset since the first elections.

On 1 June 1967, Mr. Begin joined the Government of
National Unity in which he served as Minister without Portfolio
until 4 August 1970.

On June 20, 1977, Mr. Menachem Begin, head of the Likud party—after having won the Knesset elections (17 May 1977)—presented the new Government to the Knesset and became Prime Minister of Israel.

His publications include "White Nights" (describing his wartime experience in Europe), "The Revolt", which has been translated into several languages, and numerous articles.

He is married to Aliza (nee Arnold), and has a son and two daughters.

Note: Menachem Begin died on March 9, 1992.

Source: From *Nobel Lectures, Peace 1971–1980*, Editor-in-Charge Tore Frängsmyr, Editor Irwin Abrams, World Scientific Publishing Co., Singapore, 1997. Copyright © 1978 The Nobel Foundation. Reprinted by permission.

NELSON MANDELA

Nelson Rolihlahla Mandela was born in Transkei, South Africa on July 18, 1918. His father was Chief Henry Mandela of the Tembu Tribe. Mandela himself was educated at University College of Fort Hare and the University of Witwatersrand and qualified in law in 1942. He joined the African National Congress in 1944 and was engaged in resistance against the ruling National Party's apartheid policies after 1948. He went on trial for treason in 1956–1961 and was aquitted in 1961.

After the banning of the ANC in 1960, Nelson Mandela argued for the setting up of a military wing within the ANC. In June 1961, the ANC executive considered his proposal on the use of violent tactics and agreed that those members who wished to involve themselves in Mandela's campaign would not be stopped from doing so by the ANC. This led to the formation of Umkhonto we Sizwe. Mandela was arrested in 1962 and sentenced to five years' imprisonment with hard labour. In 1963, when many fellow leaders of the ANC and the Umkhonto we Sizwe were arrested, Mandela was brought to stand trial with them for plotting to overthrow the government by violence. His

Nelson Mandela, pictured here, fought against South African apartheid for much of his life, even during his prison term of 27 years. He was awarded the Nobel Peace Prize, along with Frederik Willem de Klerk, in 1993. Mandela became the first black South African president in 1994.

statement from the dock received considerable international publicity. On June 12, 1964, eight of the accused, including Mandela, were sentenced to life imprisonment. From 1964 to 1982, he was incarcerated at Robben Island Prison, off Cape Town; thereafter, he was at Pollsmoor Prison, nearby on the mainland.

During his years in prison, Nelson Mandela's reputation grew steadily. He was widely accepted as the most significant black leader in South Africa and became a potent symbol of resistance as the anti-apartheid movement gathered strength. He consistently refused to compromise his political position to obtain his freedom.

Nelson Mandela was released on February 18, 1990. After his release, he plunged himself wholeheartedly into his life's work, striving to attain the goals he and others had set out almost four decades earlier. In 1991, at the first national conference of the ANC held inside South Africa after the organization had been banned in 1960, Mandela was elected President of the ANC while his lifelong friend and colleague, Oliver Tambo, became the organisation's National Chairperson.[13]

Source: From *Nobel Lectures, Peace 1991–1995*, Editor Irwin Abrams, World Scientific Publishing Co., Singapore, 1999. Copyright © 1993 The Nobel Foundation. Reprinted by permission.

As you can see, all three of these men took up arms against those, who, in their minds, posed a grave danger to their people. Mr. Begin wanted a new state for the Jews: Israel. After two thousand years of persecution, which resulted in the attempted Holocaust[14] of the entire European Jewish population by Hitler's Germany, Begin saw the only path to the survival of his community in the creation of a sovereign Jewish state. But, despite the Jewish historic claims to the land, Palestine was not an unpopulated area. The steady influx of the Zionists alarmed the Palestinians. The British colonial rulers found themselves in the middle of this growing conflict and were not ready to create a new state of Israel by taking land from the Arabs. As a result, Begin decided to turn to terrorism to drive out the British as well as the Arabs. To him, acts of terrorism were the only answer because the Jews did not have a conventional army to face the might of the British rulers. Instead, they could plant bombs and stage ambushes to create the maximum possible disruption in the land. Fortunately for them, the British public was weary of violence after the devastation of World War II, and thus they were in no mood to fight a long battle against the radical Jewish insurgents. Lacking public support, the British government decided to quickly grant statehood to Israel by carving out a small portion of the land and withdrawing from the region.

Although Begin and his followers succeeded in creating a sovereign state in the heart of Palestine, the new Israel created problems with their Arab neighbors. To them, it was similar to having another colonial ruler in their midst. The existing Palestinian population could not accept the loss of land that accompanied the Jewish settlement of the region. The emotions were further inflamed by the fact that Jerusalem is not only holy to Jews and Christians, it is the third holiest shrine (after Mecca and Medina) for Muslims. For them, the question of nationalism became intertwined with religious fervor.

The deepening conflict saw the emergence of Yasir Arafat

as the leader of the Palestinians, and eventually, the Palestinian Liberation Organization (PLO), the group most responsible for the Palestinian struggle for statehood. Not having an army of their own, the Palestinians resorted to terrorist attacks on Israel.

In South Africa, which was colonized by the Dutch and later seized by the British in the eighteenth century, the white population was the numerical minority, but they fully controlled the government. In the mid twentieth century, this government imposed a most unjust system called *apartheid*, which racially segregated the people of the country. In the hierarchy of races, black Africans were put at the bottom. This extreme injustice created great tensions between the races, which gave rise to conditions that might breed terrorism. Nelson Mandela gave expression to the rage of his community through a campaign of sustained violent attacks on the white regime of South Africa, and later became the head of the African National Congress (ANC). In 1990, the apartheid government, which had imprisoned Mandela for 27 years and outlawed the ANC, released Mandela and lifted the ban on the ANC. The various apartheid statutes were gradually erased from the books, and the first multi-racial elections were held in 1994. Mandela was elected president of South Africa, and he led the country through its transition from apartheid state.

So the three men became known as leaders of terrorist organizations. But how did they become "peaccmakers"? History often thrusts people in positions which, in retrospect, seem nearly unbelievable. After decades of fighting, Israel became ready to talk to the Palestinians. Menachem Begin was elected the prime minister of Israel and took the bold step toward peace with Yassir Arafat. Both men were able to set aside their deep-rooted distrust and dislike for each other and their respective people in order to start the peace process. For this, they were awarded the Noble Peace Prize. Although the process of finding peace turned out to be far more difficult than anyone anticipated

Figure 4.1 **The map above shows the state of Israel, with disputed Palestinian territories—Gaza and the West Bank—shaded darker. Israel was declared an independent state in 1948 by the United Nations. While its boundaries were originally fixed, years of conflict with its Arab neighbors led to territory shifts that contributed to Arab–Israeli tensions.**

at the time of their award, the world came to recognize the two men who took the first step.

Similarly, after the white government of South Africa gave in to domestic as well as international pressure and created a truly democratic nation, Nelson Mandela took bold steps toward reconstruction. Inspired by the works of M. K. Gandhi of India and Dr. Martin Luther King, Jr., he took an important leadership role and worked with the leader of the white government, Frederik Willem de Klerk, for a peaceful transition where everybody in South Africa could live without racial prejudice.

The course of history creates conditions in which individuals working to achieve certain goals find themselves forced to resort to tactics such as terrorism. Their actions come to be celebrated by the people on whose behalf they are fighting, which in turn propels these individuals to leadership positions. Historically, negotiations between groups of people fall to their leaders, and those who once were considered terrorists find themselves, finally, making peace.

CHAPTER 5

ISLAM AND THE WEST:
CONFLICT BETWEEN CIVILIZATIONS

It was a clear spring morning in 1995. The large imposing building was the hub of many activities because it served as the workplace for many people employed by the federal government. The building also housed a day-care center, where small children were settling down after being dropped off by their parents. Security cameras captured what happened next. The grainy pictures showed a big rental truck pulling in front of the building. There was nothing unusual about the picture, except that the truck was filled with explosives. The driver coolly climbed out of the cab, lit a fuse, and quickly entered his getaway car. After he made a turn, out of sight, he heard the deafening roar. It was 9:02 A.M. The explosion was so

When the first news came of the explosion at the Alfred P. Murrah Federal Building in Oklahoma City, above, many Americans believed that Muslim terrorists were responsible. Later, it was discovered that the perpetrators were two Americans: Timothy McVeigh and Terry Nichols.

powerful that it sheared off the entire north side of the building, killing 168 people, including many children.

The news did not come from the Middle East—the Murrah Federal building in Oklahoma City, Oklahoma, blew up as a result of a terrorist's bomb. The news brought out the worst in many. With the television news showing the carnage from car bombings in the Middle East on a daily basis, many immediately assumed that Muslim terrorists were responsible for the bombing. There were stories of ordinary citizens being harassed, simply because they "looked like Middle Eastern terrorists."

Surely, there were reasons to believe that it was Muslim religious fanatics who were behind this. Only two years before, a group linked to al Qaeda had detonated a car bomb in the underground parking structure of the World Trade Center, causing six deaths and wounding over 1,000 people. People on the streets were demanding that the U.S. government carpet bomb Middle Eastern cities. The feelings were raised to a fever pitch when a Jordanian man was arrested in London's Heathrow airport trying to flee Oklahoma City. However, the man who was arrested was Abraham Ahmed, whose only mistake was taking a flight out of Oklahoma City heading for his home in Amman, Jordan. Being the only person to have a booking for anywhere in the Middle East on that day, he was a suspect. He was arrested and brought back to the United States in handcuffs.

Fortunately for Mr. Ahmed, the actual terrorists were soon caught. They turned out to be nothing like Middle Eastern terrorists. The man who actually drove the rental truck was a decorated veteran of the Gulf War named Timothy McVeigh. On May 1, the cover of the *Time Magazine* printed the face of McVeigh superimposed over the listless body of a small child. As an incredulous America looked at the cover page, the steely eyes of the killer returned the gaze.

Why would a decorated veteran take the lives of so many of his own countrymen, women, and children and feel no regret about it? McVeigh planted the huge bomb because he believed it would start a war between blacks and whites in this country, just the way it was described in a racist novel, which inspired many white supremacist groups. In McVeigh's mind, he was certainly not a terrorist—he was part of a movement that called itself "Christian Patriots."

As we have seen, terrorism and terrorist groups can come from any part of the world. In fact, the longest surviving terrorist group, the Irish Republican Army (IRA), is a Catholic group fighting the Protestants in Northern Ireland. However, there is no denying that for the last several decades, conflict between the

Islamic nations, primarily in the Middle East, and the Western world has taken center stage. Nearly two-thirds of the terrorist groups listed in Chapter 3 operate in predominantly Islamic countries, or the group's members are mostly Muslims.

In this chapter, let's examine some of the reasons that our world often appears to be coming apart. We must understand the perspective that is allowing radicalism and anti-Americanism to spread in these parts of the world. Although a minuscule minority in the Muslim world carries out these extreme acts, there is no denying the weight of history that has caused anger to swell up to such an extent. Part of it is the inevitable outcome of two competing religions residing side by side and part of it is the legacy of the dominance of the West over the Islamic world, particularly over the past hundred years.

WORLDS APART

Soon after the death of the prophet Muhammad in the seventh century A.D., the newly founded religion of Islam spread at lightning speed to conquer nearly two-thirds of the known world, spanning from Spain to Indonesia. The inevitable outcome of the success of Islam brought it directly into a line of confrontation with the other great religion, Christianity.

Feeling threatened by the growing power in the East, the European powers responded to the call of Pope Urban II and, between 1096 and 1270, launched eight Crusades to capture the Holy Land. Although these attempts failed to keep Jerusalem in Christian hands, the bitterness from such a protracted conflict left a permanent scar in the minds of many. Although the Crusades were organized to wrest the Holy Land from the hands of the Muslims, those who joined the Crusades were less inspired by religion and, instead, were primarily interested in looting, raping, and destroying everything in their path. Even the Christians living in these areas did not escape their wrath.

We can thus understand the depth of feeling that two terms evoke on both sides of this religious divide. The word "crusade" is derived from "crucifixion" and originally meant the bearer of the cross. The definition of a crusade as "any aggressive movement for defense or advancement of an idea or cause, or against a public evil"[15] evolved later. So, after the 9/11 attacks, when President George W. Bush called the war against terrorism a "crusade," he meant a just fight against an evil. Yet, the legacy of the past defined the term in the Islamic world as an invasion from the West for pillage, rape, and murder. Quickly, the President learned of his mistake and stopped using the word.

Similarly, history has defined the term *jihad* completely differently for the two worlds. In the Islamic world, its meaning is very similar to "crusade": a struggle of the righteous ones against a tyrant or the invasion by non-believers. The meaning

Jihad:
A Brief History

In the popular press, the word *jihad* is often interpreted as "holy war." If you read the statements of radical Islamists, they are often calling fellow Muslims to join a war against their enemies. However, the proper translation of the word *jihad* is "struggle" or "striving." In the Koran, the term is used both in the military sense (as an obligation to fight against an attack by the enemies of Islam) as well as a struggle within each person to live life as an ideal Muslim. Islam is founded on five principles: faith, prayer, charity to the poor, fasting, and pilgrimage. Jihad is not one of the fundamental aspects of being a Muslim, yet it has been controversial from the beginning.

In 1258, Hulagu Khan, a Mongol chief, destroyed Baghdad with incredible cruelty. The sight of this destruction prompted a Muslim scholar named ibn Taymiyya to call for all Muslims to join the jihad against the oppressors. The concept of jihad changed in the 1920s when another Islamic scholar, Sayyid Mawdudi, exhorted Muslims to rise up against British colonial rule and establish a true Islamic country. The call to join an anti-colonial struggle changed once again, when Egyptian Muslim radicals, such as Hasan al Banna, formed the Islamic Brotherhood in the 1930s and 1940s.

of jihad has changed over the course of history, but these days, to many people in the West, the term implies terrorism inspired by religious zealots. So, you see how people can view the world through the lens of history and have two very different meanings of the same words. The terms "crusade" and "jihad," while meaning roughly the same, can raise very different emotions in different parts of the world.

The dominance of Islam lasted for over a thousand years. Islam's loss of global dominance began with the expulsion of the Moors from Spain in the fifteenth century. Since then, the rise of Western power, aided by the discoveries of the New World, ocean routes to the Orient, and the subsequent advancements in science technology, saw a steady stream of Western

However, when colonial rule effectively ended after World War II, the Islamic nations were shocked by the founding of Israel, a Jewish state established in the heart of Palestine. The inability of the leaders to prevent it added to the frustration and anger in the Arab/Muslim world. Sayyid Qutb called for jihad in the 1950s to wage a holy war. His writings shaped the concept of jihad to claim that the Arab rulers, by their timidity and association with the West, had become heretics. Therefore, it was the duty of Muslims to get rid of them and establish a nation based on the true principles of Islam.

Finally, Osama bin Laden and his fellow radicals sharpened the meaning of jihad to claim that Islam faced a threat from the polluting influences of the Western nations as well as the corrupt regimes of many Islamic rulers, particularly of Saudi Arabia. Bin Laden called the Americans the "far enemy" and other Muslim rulers who did not join him the "near enemies." He called all Muslims to join them in jihad against the two enemies, and the attacks of 9/11 were the result.*

---

* For more information, see Michael G. Knapp, "The Concept and Practice of Jihad in Islam," *Parameters: U.S. Army War College Quarterly* (Spring 2003).

victories over the Islamic empires. India fell to the British, Indonesia to the Dutch, and the Middle East and North Africa to the French and other European colonial powers. Finally, the destruction of the Ottoman Empire after World War I made the demise of Islamic dominance manifestly clear. Colonial rule added to the bitter legacy. After the end of colonial rule in the middle of the twentieth century, the Islamic world found itself fragmented, mired in poverty, and ruled by corrupt authoritarian regimes.

The final and most devastating symbol of the defeat of the Islamic power came with the establishment of Israel in 1948. The Arab countries refused to accept the Jew's Biblical claims to the land and pointed out their own historical and religious claims. After all, Jerusalem is the third holiest place in Islam after Mecca and Medina. In the subsequent wars, the Israeli defense forces, with the help of the United States, defeated the Arab forces in 1948, 1967, and 1972. Each defeat brought new frustration and anger in the Arab/Muslim world. The plight of the Palestinians in Israel became the symbol of Arab resistance. In the conflict with Israel, Arab countries do not see the United States as a neutral nation, interested in peace. Rather, the United States is viewed as a partner in the oppression of the Arabs that gives unquestioned support to the Jewish state.

The world kept changing, but this change did not favor the Islamic world. In 2002, the United Nations Development Program sponsored a group of Arab intellectual leaders, economists, political scientists, and others to do four reports on human development in the Arab countries. The first report clearly showed how the Arab world was falling behind in the race for economic and social progress.[16] The report pointed out that, despite the vast oil wealth of a number of Arab countries, their combined gross domestic product (GDP)—the value of all the goods and services produced in an economy in a given year—was less than the GDP of Spain, which is not among the wealthiest western European countries. In the following year,

Osama bin Laden:
Killing in the Name of God

Standing nearly 6' 7", Osama bin Laden, the son of one of wealthiest families of Saudi Arabia, is an imposing figure. Born in 1957, bin Laden had a religious bent from his early childhood. His father, a land developer, was one of the richest men in the world and had 52 children by various wives. Bin Laden's religious fervor only grew with age.

In 1979, the year that bin Laden graduated from a Saudi Arabian university with a degree in civil engineering, the Soviet Union invaded Afghanistan. One of the basic principles of Islam is *Umma*, or the Islamic community. Bin Laden and other Islamic fundamentalists saw the attack on Afghanistan as an attack on all Muslims. Hundreds flocked to Afghanistan to join the *jihad* against the "Godless" Soviets.

Bin Laden collected money and supplies for the mujahideen ("holy warriors"). He called his group "al Qaeda," or "the base"—the base of operations for the young men going to the Afghan battle-field. At that time, bin Laden was fighting on the same side as the United States against a common enemy. When the Soviet military was defeated—mostly by the Afghan fighters using U.S. arms and Pakistani military and intelligence support—bin Laden was quick to take credit in the name of Islam. To him, it was the strength of religious conviction that had defeated the mighty Soviet military.

The first Gulf War, in 1991, in which the United States joined other Arab countries to expel Saddam Hussein and his Iraqi army from Kuwait, disillusioned bin Laden. To him, the presence of the U.S. military in Saudi Arabia was an act of ultimate betrayal by the Saudi royal family since, to him, these were the first steps toward U.S. domination over the entire Islamic world.

Soon, an Egyptian militant and trained physician, Ayman al-Zawahiri, joined al Qaeda. Where bin Laden supplied money and inspiration, al-Zawahiri became the chief spiritual advisor and grand tactician of al Qaeda. Together, they led a number of spectacular acts of terrorism all over the world, including the 9/11 attacks.

the same group of scholars produced a report on the knowledge gap between Arab nations and a group of comparable countries. This report, which created a huge stir in the region, pointed out that the lack of freedom and the gender gap in education was retarding the immense potential for development in the Arab world.

The question of economic development has been a double-edged sword in the Arab/Muslim world. While the widening gaps create a pervasive sense of frustration among many, the process of modernization is equally suspect to a large segment of the population. As the forces of modernization forced open the doors of these traditional societies, they directly challenged the existing social, economic, and political power structures. Ideas inimical to orthodox Islam started to permeate every corner of the society. The process of modernization has always created deep conflicts all over the world, spanning history, culture, and geography. The Islamic world is no exception.

For example, when you think of modernization and progress, what kind of images come to mind? If you think about a modern society, will you not think of gleaming cities, well-dressed men and women working together, well-developed computer technology, the Internet, all the modern conveniences from fast food to shopping malls? If this is your image of a modern society, as it is for most people all over the world, you are thinking of a society far different from that imagined by traditionalists. They will point out the darker sides of Western-style "progress": the breaking down of traditional values, divorces, drug abuse, and free-for-all lifestyles that defie every law laid down by the Koran.

Today, in the large Arab cities, as in all other parts of the world, the golden arches of McDonald's compete with the spires of the old mosques. The young men and women listen to the shocking lyrics of hip-hop music, dress in immodest Western-style clothes, and otherwise pursue a lifestyle that is an affront to traditional beliefs. This is the dilemma of modernization for the Islamic world.[17]

If we are to understand the complex historical process that gave birth to the 9/11 attacks, we must do so within a broader historical, cultural, and historical perspective. Today, the two worlds of Islam and the West are increasingly divided by mutual suspicion and mistrust. If the collective frustration and anger felt by many in the Islamic world found their expression in the attacks of 9/11, we must understand their impact on U.S. foreign policies, particularly those directed toward the sources of terrorism.

In the war of words, both the worlds claim that they are the victims. The Islamic world feels that the centuries of injustice done to them have created conditions that have produced terrorism. In the West, the brutal attack on our population centers justifies our hostility and prejudice toward them. We feel justified in taking the war to Afghanistan and Iraq. As we get deeper into the confrontation, the list of victims is piling up on both sides. The sad fact is that the scar created by the spectacular attack of 9/11 is unlikely to heal anytime soon and will continue to claim victims for years, if not decades, to come.

CHAPTER 6

THE TERRORIST PROFILE

The lady at the checkout stand in my neighborhood supermarket smiled sweetly; she recognized me from the previous night's local newscast during which I was interviewed. The reporter wanted to know what kind of people terrorists are.

"What do you think of those guys?" The lady wanted to know. Before I could begin to answer the extremely broad question, she added, almost without a pause, "Let me tell you—those guys are crazy!"

How can you blame her for thinking that anyone who would kill himself in a suicide attack or take small children as hostages and threaten to blow up a building is really insane? In fact, from common folks on the street to the highest levels of political decision-makers,

Carlos the Jackal:
A Revolutionary for Hire

International terrorists sometimes create an aura of mystery, adventure, and even romance. So it was with "the Jackal." He was born in Venezuela in 1949. His father, a millionaire Marxist, named his son Ilich Ramirez Sanchez after the Russian revolutionary, Vladimir Ilich Lenin. Destined to be a terrorist, young Sanchez started early in his life when he moved to Cuba and received training from the Soviet spy agency, the KGB.

A very intelligent young man, Sanchez spoke a number of languages. Although much of his life remains shrouded in mystery, we know that he moved to London in 1966 and went to Moscow for higher studies. While in Moscow, he developed a keen interest in the Middle East conflict and, around 1970, he took his *nom de guerre*, Carlos. "Jackal" was added to his name by the media, when a police raid to one of his hideouts found a copy of the Frederick Forsyth spy novel *The Day of the Jackal*.

Carlos became a full-fledged revolutionary and was involved in a number of high-profile terrorist activities. Police suspected that he was behind the 1972 attack on the Berlin Olympic Village by Palestinian gunmen, which killed several Israeli athletes. However, the world came to know his name in 1975, when he led a team of terrorists who seized about 70 hostages during an international meeting in Vienna. Three people were killed in the attack, which resulted in the kidnapping of oil ministers from 11 nations.

Carlos, however, was inspired less by ideology than by the thrill of being a terrorist. Soon, the Palestinian groups disowned him. In the 1980s, Carlos collaborated with a number of European communist groups and carried out several bombings in Britain and France, killing dozens and wounding hundreds. Carlos became a mercenary and lent out his services to a number of Arab countries and to the Soviet Union. But, his zeal for violence and mayhem, as well his reputation for having wild parties, saw his welcome dry up. The end of the road came when he was arrested in Sudan in 1994 and handed over to the French authorities. He is currently serving a life sentence for three murders in France.

Carlos the Jackal, pictured here, was born Ilich Ramirez Sanchez. The son of a Marxist millionaire, he became interested in the Middle East conflict when he was a student in Moscow. He became known for his lust for violence and was labeled the world's most elusive terrorist.

people often claim that terrorists are, in fact, insane. For example, Senator John Warner of Virginia, the chairman of the Senate Armed Services Committee, claimed that "those who would commit suicide in their assault on the free world are not rational."

There are many psychologists, social scientists, intelligence officers, and journalists who have interviewed people arrested for terrorism or have collected information on those who have died in suicide attacks. The picture that emerges from these studies is extremely interesting—they do not show any steady pattern. If you study the profiles of inner city gang members, for instance, you will see that most of them come from poor families. They are predominantly young men, and frequently grew up with single parents. These gang members seldom completed high school.[18] When we look into the profile of terrorists, however, we find that very few generalizations hold. Let us look at what we do know about them from various studies.

POVERTY

Do terrorists come from poor families with no prospect for the future? Economists and political scientists who have looked for insight into terrorism based on poverty have found almost no link between poor countries and terrorism. For example, if you look at the world map, the poorest countries are in Africa, south Asia, and Latin America. Some of these countries do have terrorist groups, but the vast majority of terrorist groups operate out of the Middle East and even some highly developed countries.

If you want to see for yourself, on page 70, find the list of groups considered terrorists by the U.S. State Department in 2004. There are 37 terrorist groups in 19 countries (where they had their primary base in 2004). The World Bank ranks each country into four groups: low income, lower middle income, upper middle income, and high income.[19]

According to this list, most terrorist groups do not come from the poorest of the countries. In fact, many of these groups (38%) are based in upper middle and high income countries. Another 46% of terrorist groups are from

TERRORIST GOUPS ACCORDING TO THE U.S. STATE DEPARTMENT, 2004

Country (Number of Groups)	Groups	Income
Afghanistan (1)	Al Qaeda	Low income
Algeria (2)	Armed Islamic Group (GIA), Salafist Group for Call and Combat (GSPC)	Lower middle income
Colombia (3)	National Liberation Army (ELN), Revolutionary Forces of Colombia (FARC), United Self-Defense Forces of Colombia (AUC)	Lower middle income
Egypt (2)	Gama'a Islamiyya, Al-Jihad	Lower middle income
Greece (2)	Revolutionary Nuclei (RN), Revolutionary Organization 17 November (RO)	High income
Indonesia (1)	Jemmah Islamiyya	Lower middle income
Iran (1)	Mjahidin-e-Khalq	Lower middle income
Iraq (2)	Abu Nidal, Ansar al-Islam	Lower middle income
Israel (7)	Al-Aqsa Martyr Brigade, Hamas, Kahane Chai, Palestine Islamic Jihad, Palestine Liberation Front, Popular Front for the Liberation of Palestine (PFLP), PFLP General Command (PFLP-GC)	High income
Japan (1)	Aum Shinrikyo	High income
Lebanon (2)	Asbat al-Ansar, Hizbollah	Upper middle income
Pakistan (4)	Harkat al-Mujahidin, Jaish-e-Mohammed, Lashkar-e-Tayyiba, Lashkar-e-Jhangvi	Low income
Peru (1)	Shining Path	Lower middle income
Philippines (2)	Abu Sayyaf, Communist Party of the Philippines (CPP/NPA)	Lower middle income
Spain (1)	Basque Fatherland and Liberty (ETA)	High income
Sri Lanka (1)	Liberation Tigers of Tamil Elam (LTTE)	Lower middle income
Turkey (2)	Kurdistan Workers Party (PKK), Revolutionary People's Liberation Army (DHKP)	Lower middle income
United Kingdom (1)	Real IRA (RIRA)	High income
Uzbekistan (1)	Islamic Movement of Uzbekistan	Low income

lower-middle income countries and only 16% are located in low income countries.

So, if the majority of the terrorist groups are based in relatively wealthy countries, how about the terrorist themselves? Don't they turn to terrorism out of poverty and otherwise miserably impoverished lives?

When it comes to the question of individual poverty, the picture gets even more complicated. The profile of terrorists varies with each group, country, and culture. For example, consider al Qaeda: the leader of this group, Osama bin Laden, comes from one of the richest families in Saudi Arabia. He was a multimillionaire in his own right when he joined the jihadi movement. His lieutenant, Ayman al-Zawahiri, is an Egyptian doctor and was born into one of the best-known families of the country. Similarly, if you look at the men who hijacked the four airplanes on 9/11, they were all from extremely comfortable economic backgrounds.

Yet, among the rank-and-file members of al Qaeda, there are significant differences. The al Qaeda movement was joined by a large number of North African Muslims, many of them living in West European countries, primarily in France. Because of the discrimination and political isolation they faced in their host countries, their profiles do resemble our common idea of terrorists as being poor.[20] Similarly, those who have studied suicide bombers in Palestine have found similar backgrounds in poverty.[21]

EDUCATION

Since education is very closely linked to wealth (those who are affluent also tend to be better educated), we find a mixed bag when we look into the educational backgrounds of the terrorists. The Arab members of al Qaeda are highly educated. Even among the Palestinians, the level of education for those who join the various terrorist groups is higher than that of the general population.

Although it is tempting to think that terrorists are among the most poorest and most disadvantaged, the facts belie this idea. For example, Osama bin Laden, above, is from one of the wealthiest families in Saudi Arabia.

FAMILY BACKGROUND

Unlike the urban gang members in U.S. cities, the members of terrorist groups, particularly those in the Middle East and Asia, do not come from broken families. Their family values are usually extremely strong and quite often they have doting parents. Also, many of these terrorists are in steady relationships or are even married men and women with families.

Ziad Jarrah:
The Unlikely Terrorist

It was a gorgeous, sunny morning on September 11, 2001. Ziad Jarrah, a handsome young man, boarded United Airlines Flight 93. Jarrah sat in a first-class seat near the cockpit. The flight was delayed and the pilot and crew were notified of the previous hijackings that day. Within minutes of takeoff, the plane was taken over and a voice, believed to be Jarrah's, announced, "This is the captain. Would like you all to remain seated. There is a bomb on board and [we] are going back to the airport."

Among all of the 9/11 hijackers, the life of Ziad Jarrah seems the most enigmatic. He was certainly the most comfortable in the Western world and the most outgoing and fun-loving. He was better known for going to discos and beach parties than for attending mosques.

Jarrah was born to wealthy Lebanese parents, who were not particularly religious but sent their son to a private Catholic school. He met his Turkish girlfriend in 1997 and fell in love. Until the day he hijacked Flight 93, which crashed in rural Pennsylvania, he sent her e-mails nearly every day.

Unlike the other planes on 9/11, however, this one missed its target (possibly the Capitol building or the White House). Passengers on Flight 93 heard through phone calls the fates of the other hijacked planes that day. Realizing that they were going to be used as a flying bomb, they rushed the cockpit. Recognizing that their mission was in jeopardy, Jarrah coolly turned the plane upside down and, at 580 miles per hour, went into a nosedive. Everyone on board died.

Jarrah's family and friends were so shocked that they refused to believe he could ever have done it. His girlfriend filed a missing person's report. However, a detailed account of his double life left little doubt as to his role in the suicide attack.

AGE

There is another misconception that terrorists are very young, impressionable teenagers who don't know any better than to join terrorist groups, especially those who take part in suicide attacks. However, once again, the popular perception is not correct. Terrorists, as it turns out, are usually not teenagers but young adults around the age of 25.

GENDER

If you thought that terrorism is a man's job, you would be mistaken. Although in much smaller numbers, women do join terrorist groups. Because of traditional Islamic values, many Muslim groups are composed of mostly men. However, in the Middle East, women in increasing numbers are turning toward terrorism, even suicide bombings. In the Russian province of Chechnya, where an Islamic insurgency is fighting the Russian government, it is the women, known as the "Black Widows," who have carried out the majority of suicide attacks. Similarly, the Sri Lankan terrorist group LTTE has used female volunteers extensively for suicide bombings.

PSYCHOLOGICAL PROBLEMS

So far, we have seen that those who have studied the profiles of terrorists do not agree on much of anything. However, if there is one area of general agreement, it is about the psychological health of the terrorists. Extensive psychiatric examinations have shown that the vast majority of the terrorists do not show any signs of schizophrenia, depression, or any other kind of mental illness.

CHAPTER 7

GOD, GUNS, AND GANGS:
UNDERSTANDING TERRORISTS' MOTIVATIONS

"If that turns out to be true [that his sons were part of the group of the hijackers on 9/11], I'll never, never accept it from them. I'll never forgive them for [causing the disaster]."
—Mohamed Alsheri, Saudi father of Walid and Wail Alsheri, two hijackers of American Airlines Flight 11, which crashed into the North Tower of the World Trade Center[22]

The clean-shaven man, looking like an ordinary passenger, must have said his last prayer before springing into action. He was the leader of the operation and knew precisely what he had to do. He was on a mission that was not just "risky"—he knew that, for it to be successful, he would have to kill himself. Many people, including trained military officers, police, and fire fighters, routinely go into extremely hazardous jobs. But Mohammed Atta, the 33-year-old Egyptian-born man knew the difference very well. He had been preparing himself for the ultimate sacrifice. Quickly, he and his band of men took over the controls at the cockpit. The 81 passengers and crew on board heard his heavily accented false assurance: "Nobody move. Everything will be OK. If you try to make any moves,

Mohammed Atta (right) and Abdulaziz Alomari (left) are shown as they prepare to board their plane in a picture taken from an airport security camera. Atta was one of the leaders of the 9/11 plan, and he was on one of the planes that crashed into the World Trade Center.

you'll endanger yourself and the airplane. Just stay quiet." Soon after, the hijacked airplane crashed into the tower of the World Trade Center.

We've discussed the profile of the individual terrorist, but after we know who they are, we still need to know why they do it. When you decide to do something—buy a CD, play a sport, go see a movie—why do you do it? You do it because it makes you feel good. If you are studying hard, it is because that way you will be able to get the best education and, as a result, you will be able to get the job you may dream about. Most of the things that we engage in during our lives are designed to make us feel better off—have more money, more prestige, more friendship, more love, and so on.

Then there are other tasks where we do not think of ourselves, but are actions that we do for others. They can vary from small acts of kindness for a total stranger to extreme self-sacrifice (see **Self-Sacrifice: The Pat Tillman Story**, on page 83). Hearing about natural catastrophes, people donate generously. You may feel strongly about the environment, animal rights, or another cause and do things that may seriously inconvenience you or cost you money. For example, environmentalists sit in trees that they fear might be cut down by loggers. Animal rights groups stage protests or boycott certain items that they believe cause pain to animals.

We engage in such activities because we feel motivated to protect the welfare of the entire group in which we claim membership. These actions can involve quite serious acts, such as signing up for the military at times of national need, even when such actions can ultimately cause us pain, suffering, and even death. But we do it for reasons of patriotism. We do a lot of things for what psychologists call "collective identity." If we belong to a group, we take part in activities that help the group. We all engage in these kinds of actions that reflect our identity as a member of a group.

The group identity can come in many forms. Do you ever feel happy when a professional team you root for wins the championship? Or do you get sad when it loses a crucial match? If you think about it, these are professional teams, owned by billionaire owners, played by millionaire athletes. If another city offered a better deal, most teams would move. If offered a bigger salary, athletes change their teams just as quickly as they can change their uniform. Then why do you feel strongly for a professional team?

We feel strongly for any group we belong to because we are almost biologically programmed to form groups. In our evolutionary past, human beings survived by forming groups. So, group feeling comes very naturally to all of us. And when we belong to a group, we know who "we" are and who we are

Pat Tillman, former Arizona Cardinals safety, is shown here in his Army uniform. Tillman gave up a $3.6 million-dollar contract with the Cardinals to join the Army Rangers.

against. Going back to the example of rooting for a professional team, if you feel strongly for a team, it is very likely that you actually hate a rival team: "I cannot stand that team." If you feel that way, and most of us do, ask yourself the reason for your strong feelings for one team and against another. In psychology, collective identity has two parts, "us" and "them": we love those whom we consider to be like us, our friends, and hate those whom we consider our enemies.

"US" AND "THEM"

If we are to truly understand the motivations of terrorists, we must understand how these psychological forces of "us" and "them," "friend" and "foe," color our perception of the world.

Beheading: Sacrifice to Symbolism

The young man in the orange jumpsuit looked resigned to his fate, but the blurry movie clip on the Internet could not hide the sorrow and fear in his eyes. Surrounded by men wearing black clothing and masks to hide their identities, the 26 year-old perhaps sensed the inevitable outcome. The man in the center drew his knife and in front of the camera beheaded the American. The video of the brutal killing of Nicholas Berg shocked the world.

But Nick Berg was not alone in his fate. He was joined by Daniel Pearl, a *Wall Street Journal* reporter; Paul M. Johnson, Jr., a Lockheed-Martin employee; and others who were all beheaded with a sword in front of video cameras. Their lives were sacrificed to send a symbolic message, part of a macabre plot on the global stage. Since terrorism is about communicating using "propaganda by deed," the symbolism was clear. The sword occupies a special place in Islamic mythology—it is the ultimate avenger of injustice and is even featured in the flag of Saudi Arabia.

Yet, it would be a mistake to equate Islam with the barbaric acts of a few terrorists. In fact, the sword represents Islam as much as the burning crosses of the Ku Klux Klan represent the essence of Christianity. It simply portrays the same menace as the dagger for the Sicarii in ancient Palestine, or the guillotine for the Jacobins in France.

This feeling of collective identity is a source of both good and evil. It is our identifying with fellow human beings that prompts us to rise above our selfish interests and sacrifice. Yet, when it is taken to an extreme, it can make us insensitive to the pain and suffering of those we consider our enemies. Therefore, when identity with a group becomes too strong, we can become like the Nazis, who did not hesitate to send millions of innocent people to the concentration camps, or the terrorists, who knew that their actions would kill thousands but did not care.

So, to understand terrorists, you must see how they perceive the world through the lens of "us" and "them." But how do you come to see the world in that way? As we saw, it is not poverty or lack of education that makes terrorists. If it did, terrorists would come only from the poorest countries and would include only those who are the most deprived. But that is simply not the case.

If we want to know the sources of the feeling of "us" and "them" in any society, we need to look at history first. A history of injustice and grievances, which make people feel humiliated, creates the fertile ground where messages of extreme hate will grow rapidly. This hatred can be passed from one generation to the next, from grandparents and parents to children and grandchildren. For example, take the case of anti-Semitism, the way the Jews were perceived by Christians throughout history. It is not that everybody in these Christian societies felt person-ally wronged by any specific Jewish person, but rather it was the tales of their "cunning" and "deviousness" passed through generations that prejudiced people. In this case, the Biblical story of the crucifixion and the "culpability" of the Jews 2,000 years ago served as the justification for the need to punish the Jews of today.

Similarly, our discussion of the history of conflict between the Islamic world and the West can give you a good idea of how many people in the area from North Africa to Indonesia might feel about the West and how the West might view Muslims.

Suicide Bombers:
Dying to Kill

When we hear about suicide, we think of the desperate act of a psychologically depressed person, giving up life in a fit of extreme emotion. Or we think of religious fanatics blowing themselves up for the glory of God. So, we assume that those who take part in suicide attacks are either emotionally unbalanced people or lone religious zealots. Yet, careful studies show that these human bombs are in fact pawns of terrorist groups, sacrificed as a part of a calculated strategy for waging psychological warfare.

In the aftermath of the 9/11 attacks, many Americans bought copies of the Islamic holy book, the Koran, in order to better understand the terrorists. However, the religious text would be of little value, because it is not the religion that causes people to become suicide bombers—it is the terrorist leaders who use religion to justify their strategic sacrifice of human life.

When we examine the lives of those who became suicide bombers, we see that they do not fit a single profile. They are not impressionable teenagers (the average age of the 9/11 hijackers was about 28 years), nor are they religious zealots. There are many terrorists groups, such as the LTTE of Sri Lanka, who do not use any religious symbols, yet are known for their use of suicide attacks. Most of the suicide bombers are not "losers" in life, nor is there any reason to believe that they take part in these attacks out of a personal vendetta.

History clearly shows that suicide attacks are staged by terrorist organizations to achieve their political goals. We have seen that scenes of indiscriminate carnage can often change the political course of a country. In 1983, for example, two massive suicide attacks killed 241 U.S. Marines and 58 French paratroopers in Beirut, Lebanon, where they were stationed as a part of a multinational peacekeeping force. As a result of the attacks, the foreign forces were quickly withdrawn and the country descended into a bloody civil war. There are many such examples of successes of suicide attacks. From the point of view of the terrorist organizations, these are important strategic weapons, because quite often they allow these groups to achieve what they could not have achieved otherwise.

However, it is not enough to have a history—you need someone to deliver the militant message. Leaders, with their charisma and their ability to articulate in the simplest of terms the ideas of "us" and "them," have stirred people throughout history. Revolutions have sprung up, wars have been fought, and millions of people have killed or have willingly sacrificed their lives after being inspired by their leaders. Today's world of terrorism is no exception.

Among all the issues that divide the world, nothing does it more starkly than religion. While issues of ethnicity, language differences, and nationality all share in causing violence, the strict interpretation of religion paints a picture of the world in the starkest possible contrast. If one religion says that our lives should be a certain way, then any deviation from that would be disregarding those beliefs. In such circumstances, many devotees feel justified in killing all who disagree and are thus considered "evil."

Perhaps, in this rapidly changing world, many people in traditional societies feel threatened by new ideas and lifestyles that are radically different from theirs. That is why religion is increasingly taking center stage as the primary reason for terrorism, genocide, and other kinds of violence, particularly in the past decade.

For example, in 1994, nearly a third of the 49 active international terrorist groups could be classified as religious in nature or with religion as their primary motive. A year later, their number grew to be nearly half of the 56 known terrorist groups.[23] If we look at the terrorist group list for 2004, nearly two-thirds of these groups are fighting in the name of religion. They all claim to know what their God wants for the world and this gives them the blueprint by which to reshape the world. And, according to these groups, this profound transformation must be brought about by the indiscriminate use of violence.

The Islamic jihadi groups believe that they are waging a holy war against all non-believers, including those Muslims who do not share their particular interpretation of Islam. The most famous among these is, of course, al Qaeda. In their war, they target the United States and the West.

By contrast, there are religious groups that are not jihadi, which are fighting for a separate nation. These groups of terrorists, often called separatists, want a new country for themselves and are locked in a battle with their own governments. Thus, groups like Hamas are primarily interested in driving the Jews out of Israel and forming their own country, based, they claim, on the teachings of the Koran. In their fight, they do not go out of their way to target U.S. civilians or their property.

Similarly, there are two types of groups that are based solely on secular values. For example, there are several separatist groups in the world, the best known being the Tamil Tigers of

Pat Tillman:
Self-Sacrifice for a Cause

Pat Tillman was a National Football League player with a highly promising future. He walked away from a $3.6 million, three-year contract with the Arizona Cardinals for an $18,000-a-year job where his life would be in constant jeopardy. Tillman joined the Army Rangers to serve his country against an elusive and dangerous enemy in Afghanistan. He did not make his choice for the limelight—he refused every invitation for interviews after he joined the service, even refusing to meet his former teammates as a group. Nor did he consider his act particularly heroic—he often spoke of other ordinary men and women who responded to the same call of duty after the attacks of September 11, 2001. To Pat Tillman, these ordinary men and women probably endured even greater sacrifices having far less fame and fortune than he did. In April 2004, while patrolling rugged mountain trails, Tillman's platoon was ambushed and he was killed. Later investigation revealed that Tillman was killed by a dreaded accident: During a battle, "friendly fire" from members of his own platoon had taken his life.

Sri Lanka (LTTE). Sri Lanka, a teardrop-shaped island off the coast of India, has two primary ethnic groups, the Sinhalese in the south and Tamils in the north. The majority Sinhalese are mostly Buddhists, while the Tamils are Hindus. The Tamil Tigers are fighting the majority government to form their own government. Although they are Hindus, their goal is not religious.

Also among the secular groups are those inspired by communist ideologies. Through their struggle, these groups want to form a country based on Marxist principles of equality and no private property. While some of these groups are not fighting the United States and the West, such as the Communist Party of the Philippines (CPP), there are others who deliberately target the United States and its economic interests. These groups include the Turkish Revolutionary People's Liberation Army/Front (DHKP/C) and the two Greek communist groups.

However, don't think that all terrorists are motivated by religious faith or some other deep ideological beliefs. While human beings are deeply influenced by groups, there is also another very important set of motivations—our own selfish interests. There are many terrorist groups that claim lofty goals but are in reality nothing more than gangs of criminals. They are only interested in making money through their terrorist activities. For example, the Abu Sayyaf group of the Philippines claims to be an Islamic jihadi group, but in fact is a criminal gang interested in making money by taking hostages for ransom. Similarly, the Colombian group FARC calls itself a Marxist communist group, yet they are deeply involved in the drug trade. So you see, viewed from the perspective of motivations, there is not much difference between these groups and the ordinary street gangs that terrorize the inner cities of our country.

CHAPTER 8

HOW PEOPLE BECOME TERRORISTS

You may have seen it in the movies: An innocent person is captured by an evil group—in the 1960s and 1970s, Hollywood's favorite villains were the communist intelligence agencies—and becomes a weapon in the hands of an evil genius through brainwashing. In the movies, the human robot is instructed to carry out a diabolical plan, but somehow the world is saved when the hero foils the plot and the victim is awakened from the grip of mind control.

The idea of "brainwashing" or "mind control" plays a prominent role in the public discussion of terrorism. The reason is that we can readily understand actions that benefit an individual: We understand why people would work hard and do well in business, sports, or academics. We can also easily recognize the motivation behind becoming

A Palestinian child wearing a headband that says "Jerusalem for us" holds a real gun during an anti-Israeli demonstration in Lebanon.

a bank robber or perhaps a corrupt official. However, being from a society that places the utmost importance on individualism, we often have difficulty accepting that rational people would actually engage in actions that can put one's personal welfare and even one's own life in jeopardy. Yet, throughout history, people have sacrificed their lives and liberty for the sake of their chosen groups.

If you want to understand why people join terrorist groups, you must not think of them as crazy or "brainwashed." Instead, look for the construction of their group-based mindset that prompts them to become terrorists. At this time, you should also know that not all terrorists are inspired by ideology or the desire to undertake selfless acts for the sake of their group. There are many who join terrorist groups only from their own selfish considerations—making money, looting, raping, or to be powerful in their communities, often by simply being able to carry a semi-automatic weapon. In fact, there are many groups that, despite their rhetoric of higher goals, are nothing but

Joining Jihad

How do people become members of a terrorist organizations? Do these organizations send out recruiters like the U.S. military? Do they visit high schools and college campuses to recruit young men and women to their cause?

There are many different kinds of terrorist groups. Let us see how a "movement" such as the global jihadi movement can spread. Terrorist organizations do not go out and recruit people off the street. The primary reason is that if they did, their groups would be easily infiltrated by police and intelligence officers. Instead, these secretive organizations get their foot soldiers through kinship and other social affiliations. Quite often, people join because they had an older brother, cousin, or some other relative already in the organization.

The second way of joining these groups is through friendship. A small group of people, connected through social bonds, form a cell. Soon, one of them may find a "bridge" or a contact to a higher level of insider of the terrorist group. The members of a cell can get instructions regarding an operation and get money and other kinds of logistical support from this higher level "node."

Take for instance the Hamburg cell of al Qaeda, which helped carry out the 9/11 attacks. Nine men from a number of Arab countries attended services at a neighborhood mosque and most of them were studying at a local technical college. They were drawn together by their need to associate with others with a similar background and found themselves united in their anger against the West. They were inspired by the actions and words of Osama bin Laden. Soon, their contacts provided them with money and instructions to carry out the 9/11 attacks.*

---

* For more information, see Marc Sageman, *Understanding Terror Networks*. Philadelphia: University of Pennsylvania Press, 2004.

criminal gangs, such as the Abu Sayyaf in the Philippines and the FARC in Colombia.

How do people join these terrorist groups? If you look at how most terrorist groups operate, they do not have a recruiting department. When you look for a job, you can either find out who is hiring or can look up the "help wanted" ads from prospective employees. However, for obvious reasons, the terrorist groups do not advertise, and they don't have to.

At certain times in history, societies become awash with a certain ideology, the same way that fashions change what we can buy from stores. For example, if you grew up in certain parts of Northern Ireland, your religion—whether you are a Protestant or Catholic—would define who you are in the society. In such circumstances, babies would grow up with what a prominent psychiatrist, Jerrold Post, calls "hatred bred in bones." If you walk down the mean streets of Belfast and Londonderry, you will see that children from their infancy are brought up in hatred toward the others. On the streets, huge murals of each faction's heroes urge passersby to join the fight and pictures of past atrocities instill deep anger. In such societies, a group mentality of collective identity sets in, where you clearly know who you are and who your enemies are. So powerful are these images that studies show that young children learn to distinguish between a "Catholic look" and a "Protestant look." It may seem amazing to an outsider, but in a deeply divided society like Northern Ireland, even a child can look at a person and guess his or her religion.

If you were living in parts of the Islamic world, you would constantly see television programs, read newspaper accounts, and hear speeches made by political and religious leaders detailing the effects of Israeli military action on the lives of ordinary Palestinians, but virtually no information about the victims of suicide attacks. In contrast, if you lived in Israel, on television you would mostly see the horrendous chaos created by suicide attacks but almost nothing of the anguish of the victims of

While the Protestants in Belfast celebrate the Orange March on July 12, the little boy on the left shows his patriotic pride by donning a hat with the British flag printed on it. On the right, a Catholic girl runs through the deserted streets under the sign "Brits Out, Not Sell Out." Those of us who are on the outside may wonder how the two children will see other when they grow up.

Israeli attacks. Visit any part of the world wracked by sectarian violence and you will see similar pictures of biased perceptions caused by partisan news coverage. Under such conditions, a

When Hatred Is Bred in the Bones

The entire city shakes in anticipation of the parade. On one side of the city, neighborhood groups and fraternity lodges prepare floats, street corners are freshly painted in patriotic colors, children wear their best clothes, and the smell of freshly-cooked hotdogs hangs heavily over the celebrating crowd. On the other side of the city, people try to look the other way. They close down their businesses, and those who can afford a vacation leave town. The deserted roads and shuttered storefronts show the unmistakable division. After all, this is no ordinary parade. Nor is it an ordinary town.

It is the Orangemen March, celebrated on July 12 in Belfast, Ireland. No year in Irish history is better known than 1690. No Irish battle is more famous than Protestant William of Orange's victory over Catholic James II at the River Boyne. Although history is ambiguous about the extent of religious devotion that brought the two adversaries to their fateful encounter, their images are used as focal points of sectarian pride and disdain for the enemy. The parade carries the unmistakable demonstration of threat, replete with muscular men brandishing swords and muskets, ready to take up arms for their cause. The night before, Protestant neighbor-hoods erect huge bonfires where the national flag of the Catholic Irish Republic is ceremoniously put to flame. Each year, the age-old conflict between the Catholics and Protestants in North-ern Ireland—euphemistically known as the "troubles"—flares up like clockwork. Each year, the evening news dutifully reports how many people are killed and injured in that day's inevitable violence.

In a city where everybody wants to know each other's religious affiliation (and hence, political orientation), no clue is missed. In order to survive one must be able to distinguish between a friend and a foe. Psychologists report that children from an early age learn to rec-ognize a "Catholic look" and a "Protestant look." The way someone is dressed, the way certain words are spoken, or the way the names are spelled are dead giveaways. In Belfast and others towns around the world, where sectarian hatred seethes beneath a none-too-opaque a veil, mutual hatred comes with mother's milk. Noted psychologist Jerrold Post calls this hatred "bred in the bones."

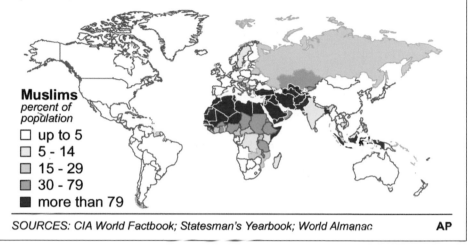

Muslim populations worldwide

Islam is the second-largest religion in the world, with more than 1.1 billion followers. A large Muslim population is concentrated in the Middle East and North Africa, but there are more than 5 million practicers in the United States.

Muslims
percent of population

- ☐ up to 5
- ☐ 5 - 14
- ☐ 15 - 29
- ☐ 30 - 79
- ■ more than 79

SOURCES: CIA World Factbook; Statesman's Yearbook; World Almanac   **AP**

Figure 8.1 The map above demonstrates that Muslims are not only from the Middle East. In the same way, a person who is Muslim, or Middle Eastern, is not automatically a terrorist.

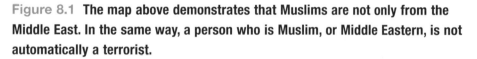

terrorist group does not have to advertise or even seek out prospective members. They come in by the droves to join the groups. The terrorist groups, in turn, pick only those who are truly dedicated or have specific talents or knowledge that the group might need for its operation.

The groups that operate and recruit from within a society have a somewhat easier task than those that are located in distant lands. For example, if you look at how the 9/11 hijackers came to join al Qaeda, you will discover that many of them were members of small groups, called "cells" in intelligence terminology, in the German port city of Hamburg. When former CIA official Marc Sageman tracked the process by which they joined al Qaeda, he found out that these Arab men felt homesick in an

John Walker Lindh, a young man from California, attended a madrassah (or Islamic school) in Pakistan, as demonstrated on this attendance register from the school. There, he went by the Muslim name "Suliman," which is listed second in the register.

alien culture far away from their homes. So, they were looking for a place where they could meet others of similar background and have their national foods. The mosques in Hamburg

Terrorism and the Internet

The men in the car were frustrated. They were driving down the streets of Casablanca, in Morocco, and they wanted to kill. Their job was to plant five bombs throughout the city timed to go off at the same time, killing and injuring as many as they possibly could. But they did not have luck on their side. They did not get proper training. Unlike their more seasoned fellow jihadis, they did not go to Afghanistan and instead were trained over a couple of weekends in the nearby caves. The bombs were too bulky and unreliable. The instructions from al Qaeda leadership were scanty at best. So, they had to search the Internet and finish building the explosives the day before. For fear of being detected, they could not even get proper directions to their attack sites.

Finally, when they placed and detonated the explosives, four went off, killing only the terrorists. The fifth one killed at least 31 people and injured many more, marking May 16, 2003, as one of the bloodiest in the history of the North African nation. The ringleaders of the attacks were quickly apprehended by the Moroccan police.

The story illustrates the problems of communication for the terrorist cells and their leadership. When the mujahideen went to Afghanistan in the early 1990s, they complained about the isolation they felt without phones or other communication devices. However, technology soon came to their aid. Through various Websites, chat rooms, and e-mail, the terrorists could not only spread their messages and be part of the global jihadi community, they could also download the necessary information for making bombs. Osama bin Laden invested in a satellite phone and can be seen using it in the mountains of Afghanistan in television footage.

However, new technology can be a double-edged sword. The use of these devices gave law enforcement officials a unique opportunity to detect the terrorists. Laptops and other computers could be analyzed for files that the user thought had been completely deleted. So, although the Internet and other high-tech communication devices have made it possible for the terrorists to develop global organizations, their use has also allowed intelligence agencies to track them down as the terrorists and their pursuers play a continuing cat-and-mouse game.

offered such a place. They were also drawn together by their bonds of kinship with others from the same families or tribal origins. When they came to worship in a certain mosque, they made their own circle of friends, their small cell. They were also united by their hatred of the United States and Israel. Day after day, the slanted news would deepen their anger into a single-minded obsession. Soon, either by chance or through conscious seeking, they made contact with one of the top operatives of al Qaeda. After the contacts were made, the plan of attack started to take shape.

Some people became involved with al Qaeda and their supporters, the Taliban government of Afghanistan, through their own initiatives. For example, look at the case of John Walker Lindh, a 20-year-old man from California, who was captured while fighting for the Taliban against the U.S. military. As a shy young man of 16, Lindh was seeking a religious experience when he embraced Islam. Apparently, it was the autobiography of black Muslim leader Malcolm X that inspired him. In 1998, Lindh went to the Middle East to learn Arabic and become an Islamic scholar. Two years later, he went to Pakistan and, in 2001, he was recruited by the Pakistan-based radical Kashmiri group Harkat-ul-Mujahidin. He was then sent to Afghanistan, where he was finally caught by the advancing U.S. Army.[24]

The following article from the Los Angeles Times shows how one family man was spurred to action by the images he saw on his television.

Getting an Education in Jihad

BEKAA VALLEY, Lebanon—The handsome, 35-year-old teacher had many things to live for—a PhD, a steady job, a healthy salary—but still he decided to leave home, make his way to Syria and then sneak over the border into Iraq, intent on fighting Americans, even if it meant dying in a suicide attack.

In the beginning, the schoolteacher had struggled to decide how he felt about the U.S.-led invasion of Iraq. It spelled humiliation and sorrow to Arabs. But as an Arab who had tasted the despair of despotism, he had a small spot of hope.

"At first, I thought, 'OK, the Americans want to bring democracy to the region,' " he said.

That was before he turned on the television to the grainy images of prisoner abuse at Abu Ghraib. "The human triangle. The woman dragging the man by the leash," said the teacher, a broad man with a clipped beard and intense gaze. "These images affected me deeply. The shame the Americans brought. I was fervently monitoring the TV images, not so much the words as the pictures."

He remembered that President Bush called the war on terrorism a "crusade." He thought about American helicopters being used by the Israeli army to attack Palestinians. And he decided that sitting impotently in Lebanon wasn't enough.

Over dates and sweet coffee in a middle-class living room here, he recently spoke in measured tones about his fervor to fight on behalf of Muslims against U.S. troops—and his decision to leave the battle in Iraq to make his way home again.

The story of the teacher, who spoke on the condition that neither he nor his hometown be named, reflects the oft-stated notion that the war in Iraq has opened a regional Pandora's box of jihad. In a region where so many people feel helpless before repressive governments and U.S. policy, the road to Iraq has become a trail of independence in the minds of some men, a way for young Muslims to come of age and to join the battles they see on television.

His journey began here, in a high valley that is so flat it looks like it was ironed, stretching like a gritty carpet between the mountains of southern Lebanon, hard against the Syrian border. Unemployment is rife and religious zeal intense.

It is a hardscrabble place where international worries and local woes are intimately intertwined. A recent Friday sermon called for martyr's blood to avenge the Iraqi insurgent shot dead on the floor of a mosque by a U.S. Marine. "Every day we are seeing these things and hearing the same word: Fallouja," the preacher cried. "What are we supposed to tell our men? To put down their weapons? To surrender? If we do, who's going to avenge their blood and tears?"

Then the sermon shifted seamlessly; the preacher tried to drum up donations to heat the schools. "We worry about Iraq and about Palestine," he said, "but it's getting cold here."

This ancient strip of farms has a history of defiance, and it has sent its share of men to join the insurgency in Iraq. Some made their way back home. Others have been commemorated at funerals without corpses after friends called from Iraq to report their deaths.

Martyrdom doesn't come cheap. Foreign fighters are expected to pay their own way, from smugglers' fees to meals. Many of the would-be mujahedin, or holy warriors, simply can't afford to go, said Shaaban Ajani, the mayor of a town in the Bekaa called Majdal Anjar.

Within Iraq, there is broad consensus that foreign fighters form only a small band of the insurgency roiling the country. Nevertheless, in neighboring countries the psychological resonance of the struggle, and the adulation and envy of the foreign jihadis, has been profound.

"If a man stands just an hour with a weapon in his hand to fight jihad, it's better than being a preacher in Mecca for 100 years," the teacher said. "It's not about preaching. It's about actions."

Ajani, the mayor, doesn't disguise the pride in his voice when he tells a visitor that two men from his town were killed fighting in Iraq. "It is noble, and it's a religious duty," he said.

In his town, tensions between a frustrated people and their national government exploded this fall. Lebanese agents swept through the Bekaa, carrying out a sting operation on what was described as an Al Qaeda cell.

Ten people were arrested. One, a Majdal Anjar resident named Ismail Mohammed Khalil, 32, died in custody shortly after his arrest. The government said he'd suffered a heart attack. Witnesses said his body came home covered with cigarette burns, bruises and scorch marks left by electrical shocks.

In the Bekaa, Khalil is remembered as a mild-mannered man who sold used cellphones to support his five children. After his body was returned, hundreds of men took to the streets and rioted. The suspect's real crime, his neighbors and family say, was sympathy for the mujahedin who trekked to Iraq—and his fervent hope that he could someday afford to join their ranks.

"America has declared war against the Sunni people," said the mufti of the Bekaa, Khalil Mais. "Are Muslims forbidden to defend themselves? Jihad is the defense of country and of honor. How can you watch television every night and not go?"

It was that conviction that inspired the schoolteacher to make his way to Iraq.

After he decided to go, he waited for a break in classes. It was a quick bus ride to Syria. He set off in the spring with a shortwave radio, a small bundle of clothes and some cash.

The teacher had collected $3,500 for his trip. It was all the money he'd saved from his salary, and he feared that it wouldn't be enough to keep him going for what he expected would be a long period of fighting. He had a local connection, a friend from the Bekaa who had joined foreign fighters in Iraq and had agreed to vouch for him.

He remembers standing, on a cold spring night, on the line between Syria and Iraq. Four border-jumpers before him had been caught by Syrian troops. The smuggler he'd hired to ferry him to Baghdad was edgy. They would hike through the desert rather than chance the roads.

It was a starless night, the teacher recalls, and he hadn't expected the desert to be so cold. Stray dogs roamed the sands; American helicopters thrummed overhead. He didn't let his guide rest or smoke cigarettes for fear of getting caught.

The schoolteacher walked all night through the Iraqi desert until he reached the outskirts of a small town. The guide walked toward the lights and fetched a truck while the teacher waited in the wastelands. Then they drove into Baghdad to meet a contact beneath a downtown bridge.

He was taken to a villa crowded with dozens of men from Yemen, Libya, Algeria, Syria and a host of other Arab countries. They'd order out for food, and when it arrived, they'd argue over who would pay.

"It was a very nice atmosphere. Nobody wanted to take anything; everybody wanted to give," the teacher said. "If there was a household chore to be done, we fought over it."

Most of the men seemed well-educated, and they didn't lack for cash. Some of them were veterans of the battle against U.S. Special Forces and their Afghan allies in Tora Bora, Afghanistan. At night, they'd sit in the villa, which was furnished with only a handful of chairs, and talk about the sort of government that the Islamic people would install once they kicked out the Americans.

After about eight days, it was the teacher's turn to move. They took him to Fallouja in a battered car. He believed the time for his suicide mission was near, but he ended up in another house, surrounded by Saudis—mostly Salafists, adherents of the most rigorous school of Islamic thought—who were waiting eagerly for their own suicide missions. The men were organized into platoons, the teacher said, with every 50 or so foot soldiers under the guidance of a commander.

"Many of the guys in the house had very limited military training," he said. "But it doesn't take much military training to get in the car and blow yourself up."

The teacher spoke reverently of Jordanian-born militant Abu Musab Zarqawi, who has been tied to numerous beheadings and other deadly attacks in Iraq. He bragged that he spent a night with a Zarqawi aide who has since been killed and that he caught a glimpse inside a spartan bedroom occupied by Zarqawi. Though he didn't see the militant leader, he described the Jordanian kaffiyeh, or headdress, he left behind.

After a week of waiting around in Fallouja, the teacher said, he began to feel guilty. It wasn't that he became frightened, but the dreams he'd had in Lebanon didn't match the mundane reality in Iraq. He felt more like an interloper than a savior.

"I realized I was staying in somebody's house, and the owners were moving from place to place to make room for us," he said. "Then I realized they didn't need us, and in fact we were sort of hampering the Iraqis."

The foreigners' accents made them a security threat, and their makeshift dormitories drew U.S. bombs to residential neighborhoods. Iraqi collaborators with the U.S.-led forces would throw compact discs onto rooftops to mark the homes where the mujahedin were sleeping for U.S. warplanes, the teacher said.

"We were a burden, and the Iraqis could take up the battle," the teacher said. "I came to realize that they didn't need people, they needed money much more than people. I realized I'd be of greater use if I financially supported them."

He made his way back through the desert under a moon that was nearly full. American patrols swooped overhead. At the border, he said, he spent $200 bribing Syrian officials to let him pass.

Now he is home, among friends envious of his adventure. He has occasional regrets about returning to Lebanon.

Other men from the Bekaa also have come home, community leaders said. But the humiliation that drove them into the desert continues to fester, given in regular doses by the evening news.

"When I saw the man shot in the mosque, I wanted to go back," the teacher said with a shrug. "They say it's a war crime. I think the whole war is a war crime."

The sad part of human nature is that all of the people we have come to regard as terrorists were not born with any specific genetic structure that caused them to join terrorist organizations. Some join because of circumstances—where they are born, who they are—while others do so because they become inspired by people like Osama bin Laden. These are ordinary people, no different from any of us. We all have the potential to do good or to bring death and destruction. When it comes to terrorism, it all depends on how we perceive the world and what we choose to do about it.

CHAPTER 9

FIGHTING TERRORISM

There is a huge gap in the skyline of New York City where the Twin Towers used to soar to the sky. As the nation rebuilds and moves forward, the hurt will remain like an empty space in our hearts for generations to come. As we watched the 9/11 attacks with amazement and horror, most of us were filled with questions: How do we respond to this atrocity? How do we look at our neighbors in the Islamic countries? How many of our individual liberties should we sacrifice to fight the menace of terrorism?

In the aftermath of the attack, President George W. Bush declared a war on terrorism. He promised a nation thirsting for justice that he would pursue the terrorists to the ends of the Earth.

As we faced the threat of attacks by an unseen enemy, there was a renewed effort to learn more about terrorism.

From the gathered evidence, it seems clear that, when it comes to terrorism, "war" might not the right metaphor to use. In a war, we have a definite enemy and an organized government against which we can send in our military forces. Yet, terrorism is different: The enemy is elusive, it hides among civilian populations and strikes only when we are not paying attention. So, if we go after the terrorists with our full military might, we often destroy innocent lives. The biggest source of terrorists' power is their support among the people they are supposed to represent. When we alienate people through civilian "collateral damage," the support base for the terrorists increases.

Yet, when we don't allow our rage to overwhelm reason, we realize the trap that the terrorists set for us. We cannot ignore those who murder our citizens and destroy our property, so we must go after them militarily. Yet, if we overreact and unjustly punish those who are not responsible, if we think that everybody who lives in the area is our enemy, then we only play into the hands of the terrorists. Indiscriminate acts of revenge only strengthen the terrorist organizations and their resolve to hurt us.

As we mourn the dreadful day of September 11, 2001, we must realize that what we are fighting is not so much an individual, such as Osama bin Laden, or even a group, such as al Qaeda or the Taliban—what we are fighting in the global arena is an idea. Ideas, not simply a list of grievances alone, have moved people throughout history. The minutemen during the American Revolution, the volunteers in the Spanish Civil War, the Communist sympathizers in support of Che Guevara, and the Freedom Riders in the United States going to the South to register blacks to vote have all been moved by the strength of ideas. Some ideas have advanced what we generally uphold as humanity, others have caused pain and misery.

Today, we face the menace of an idea that holds out promises of an Islamic paradise on Earth to many who are haunted by an overwhelming feeling of losing out. The once proud Islamic movement that spanned the known world is now reduced to a number of mostly insignificant countries, many

Abu Ghraib:
A Gift to the Terrorists' Cause

In the era of Saddam Hussein, Abu Ghraib, located 20 miles west of Baghdad, was one of the world's most notorious prisons, where torture, executions, and awful living conditions were the daily routine. After the fall of Saddam's regime, Abu Ghraib became a U.S. military prison. As the coalition forces faced stiff Iraqi resistance, the prison soon filled with prisoners, most of whom (including women and teenagers) were civilians. Many of them had been picked up in random military sweeps and at highway checkpoints. The prisoners were classified in three categories: common criminals; security detainees suspected of "crimes against the coalition"; and a small number of suspected "high-value" leaders of the insurgency.

Janis Karpinski, an Army Reserve brigadier general, was named commander of the 800th Military Police Brigade and put in charge of military prisons in Iraq. General Karpinski was a decorated officer, but had no training in handling prisoners. The reservists who were in charge of the overcrowded prison similarly had very little training as prison guards.

Stories of rampant abuse of detainees started circulating and then a few photos were leaked to the media showing the torture and humiliation of Iraqi prisoners. Their plight has become a source of embarrassment for the U.S. forces and a potent recruiting tool for those fighting the coalition forces. Although General Karpinski was demoted and several Army reservists faced trial, the damage had been done. All over the Muslim world, Abu Ghraib has become a symbol of U.S. injustice and a gift to the recruiters of terrorist organizations.

wracked by poverty, injustice, and feelings of desperation. Although poverty per se does not cause terrorism, it supplies the essential foundation on which leaders of terrorist groups can build their message of hate. It is not just economic poverty that causes terrorism—it is the poverty of opportunity, political freedom, and a global outlook. It is the poverty of basic human dignity that shapes those who consider the only way of affirming their own lives is by ending the lives of others with a spectacular show of violence and destruction.

Terrorism's Trap

Terrorists lay their trap and wait. This has been their mode of operation from the earliest known examples of terrorism. The Sicarii did it 2,000 years ago, just as the terrorists do all over the world today. In their attacks, they not only ambush those who are killed or wounded, they also snag an entire nation through their outrageous acts.

Their violence is not simply directed at their immediate victims—in planning these attacks, they aim at much larger prey. The scenes of death and destruction—of innocent people or symbols of societies—ultimately challenge us to come down to their level. They win when in our rage we demand retribution and violate the rules of law on which our societies are founded. Since they melt away in the community and do not face the police or military, our anger gets directed at every member of the community from which they come.

A terrorist group's strength is measured by the amount of support they get from their community. If the community support weakens, the terrorist organizations become weak; if it gets stronger, so does the organization. Therefore, the terrorists invite overreaction from their opponents. They love nothing more than when our actions anger their base of support. That's why acts of terrorism look like the work of mad men. But the moment we react in indiscriminate anger, we fall into their trap.

When hate threatens our lives and the roots of our civilization, we must fight back, not just against the leaders or their organizations but against the ideas they preach. In our battle, we wage war not against the entire Islamic world, but the idea that a particular brand of Islam should rule the world.

How do we fight this war of ideas? We can overthrow a tyrannical regime with our military forces, but how do we win over those who hate us more than they love their own lives? The policy that confirms the worst about us only adds fuel to the fires of hatred. Every military action that kills innocent bystanders, regardless of the nobility of the intention, gives birth to more suicide bombers. Every time the pictures of prisoners being abused and humiliated by the members of our armed forces are broadcast, the ranks of terrorists swell.

In the war of ideas, we should know that Western civilization is rooted in the concept of the rule of law. We cannot win over those who violate the law by breaking the law ourselves. Any act that violates the basic principles on which our civilization is based ultimately makes us weak. Any move that weakens our friendship with other countries isolates us, because if there is a solution to the problem of terrorism, we must seek it through cooperating with other nations. This does not mean that we should coddle those who attack us. We should take every action to defeat terrorists, militarily, politically, and most importantly, ideologically.

History tells us that fighting terrorism is a long-term proposition and we must be prepared for a long struggle. However, as we pursue those who have caused such incredible harm to innocent civilians, we must know who the terrorists really are. In our fight against terrorism, it is important to know what we are fighting against, but it is even more important to know what we are fighting for.

Chapter 1
What Is Terrorism?

1 For an excellent discussion, see Bruce Hoffman, *Inside Terrorism*. Columbia University Press, 1998. Also, for a history of terrorism, see Walter Laqueur, *Terrorism*. London: Weidenfield and Nicolson, 1977.

2 Simon Schama, *Citizens: A Chronicle of the French Revolution*. New York: Vantage Books, 1989, p. 702.

3 Alex P. Schmid and Jenny de Gaff, *Violence as Communication: Insurgent Terrorism and the Western News Media*. Beverly Hills, CA: Sage Publications, 1982.

4 Daniel J. Goldhagen, *Hitler's Willing Executioners: Ordinary Germans and the Holocaust*. New York: Alfred A. Knopf, 2000.

5 Alex P. Schmid, *Political Terrorism: A Research Guide*. New Brunswick, NJ: Transaction Books, 1984. Also see Alex P. Schmid, Alberto Jongman, et al., *Political Terrorism: A New Guide to Actors, Authors, Concepts, Data Bases, Theories, and Literature*. New Brunswick, NJ: Transaction Books, 2005.

6 Section 140(d)(2) of the Foreign Relations Authorization Act, Fiscal Years 1988 and 1989. See "Foreign Terrorist Organizations," U.S. State Department Website: http://www.state .gov/s/ct/rls/fs/2004/12389.htm.

Chapter 2
Terrorism in History

7 James Forman, *Anarchism: Political Innocence or Social Violence?* New York: F. Watts, 1975. Also see Paul Avrich, *Anarchist Portraits*. Princeton, NJ: Princeton University Press, 1988.

8 David Rapoport, "Four Waves of Modern Terrorism," in Audry Kurth Cronin and James D. Ludes (eds.), *Attacking Terrorism: Elements of a Grand Strategy*. Washington, D.C.: Georgetown University Press, 2004, p. 61.

Chapter 3
Terrorist Groups

9 See "Foreign Terrorist Organizations," U.S. State Department Website: http://www.state.gov/s/ct/rls/fs/2004/ 12389.htm. There are other Websites of various research institutes that can also give you detailed decriptions of these and many other groups. For instance, see: SITE Institute (http://www.siteinstitute.org/terrorist-groups.html) or International Policy Institute for Counter-Terrorism (http://www.ict.org.il).

10 This group is also known as Fatah Revolutionary Council, Arab Revolutionary Brigades, Black September, and Revolutionary Organization of Socialist Muslims. See "Terrorist Group Profiles: Abu Nidal Organization," U.S. Navy Website: http://library.nps .navy.mil/home/tgp/abu.htm.

11 Although there are numerous books and articles on the problems of Ireland, for a concise review of the history, look at the BBC's Website: "Wars and Conflict: The Troubles." Available online at http://www.bbc.co .uk/history/war/troubles/index.shtml.

Chapter 4
Terrorist Leaders or Peacemakers?

12 The place of Arafat's birth is disputed. Besides Cairo, other sources mention Jerusalem and Gaza as his birthplace.

13 For more updated biographical information, see: Nelson Mandela, *Long Walk to Freedom: The Autobiography of Nelson Mandela*. Boston: Little, Brown, 1994.

14 The word Holocaust is a combination of two words: "Holo", which in Greek means "total," and "caustos," meaning "destruction" or "burnt."

Chapter 5
Islam and the West:
Conflict Between Civilizations

15 *New Webster's Dictionary of the English Language*, Deluxe Encyclopedic Edition. Springfield, MA: Merriam-Webster, 1981, p. 243.

16 United Nations Human Development Program Website: http://hdr.undp.org/.

17 Benjamin R. Barber, *Jihad vs. McWorld: How Globalism and Terrorism are Reshaping the World*. New York: Times Books/Random House, 1995.

Chapter 6
The Terrorist Profile

18 C. Ronald Huff (ed.), *Gangs in America*. Newberry Park, CA: Sage Publications, 1990.

19 You can see the complete list of countries at the World Bank Website: http://www.worldbank.org/data/countryclass/classgroups.htm#Low _income.

20 See Marc Sageman, *Inside Terror Networks*. Philadelphia: University of Pennsylvania Press, 2004.

21 Jerrold M. Post, *Leaders and Their Followers in a Dangerous World: The Psychology of Political Behavior*. Ithaca, NY: Cornell University Press, 2004.

Chapter 7
Gods, Guns, and Gangs:
Understanding Terrorists' Motivations

22 Dafna Linzer, "9/11 One Year Later," *Chicago Sun-Times* Special Edition (September 8, 2002). Available online at http://www.suntimes.com/special_sections/ sept11/attacks/thehijackers.html.

23 Hoffman, *Inside Terrorism*, p. 91.

Chapter 8
How People Become Terrorists

24 John Walker Lindh was sentenced to 20 years of imprisonment on October 4, 2002. See Richard D. Mahoney, *Getting Away with Murder: The Real Story Behind American Taliban John Walker Lindh and What the U.S. Government Had to Hide*. New York: Arcade Publishers, 2004.

Avrich, Paul. *Anarchist Portraits.* Princeton, NJ: Princeton University Press, 1988.

Barber, Benjamin R. *Jihad vs. McWorld: How Globalism and Terrorism are Reshaping the World.* New York: Times Books/Random House, 1995.

Forman, James. *Anarchism: Political Innocence or Social Violence?* New York: F. Watts, 1975.

Gupta, Dipak K. "Roots of Terrorism." In Tore Bjorgo (ed.). *Root Causes of Terrorism.* London: Routledge, 2005.

Hoffman, Bruce. *Inside Terrorism.* New York: Columbia University Press, 1998.

Huff, C. Ronald (ed.). *Gangs in America.* Newberry Park, CA: Sage Publications, 1990.

Laqueur, Walter. *Terrorism.* London: Weidenfeld and Nicholson, 1977.

Linzer, Dafna. "9/11 One Year Later." *Chicago Sun-Times* Special Edition (September 8, 2002). Available online at http://www.suntimes.com/ special_sections/sept11/attacks/thehijackers.html.

Mahoney, Richard D. *Getting Away with Murder: The Real Story Behind American Taliban John Walker Lindh and What the U.S. Government Had to Hide.* New York: Arcade Publishers, 2004.

Post, Jerrold M. *Leaders and Their Followers in a Dangerous World: The Psychology of Political Behavior.* Ithaca, NY: Cornell University Press, 2004.

Rapoport, David. "Four Waves of Modern Terrorism." In Audry Kurth Cronin and James D. Ludes (eds.). *Attacking Terrorism: Elements of a Grand Strategy.* Washington, D.C.: Georgetown University Press, 2004, pp. 46–73.

Sageman, Marc. *Inside Terror Networks.* Philadelphia: University of Pennsylvania Press, 2004.

Schama, Simon. *Citizens: A Chronicle of the French Revolution.* New York: Vantage Books, 1989.

Schmid, Alex P., and Berto Jongman. *Political Terrorism: A Research Guide.* New Brunswick, NJ: Transaction Press, 1984.

Schmid, Alex P., and Berto Jongman. *Political Terrorism: A New Guide to Actors, Authors, Concepts, Data Bases, Theories, and Literature.* New Brunswick, NJ: Transaction Press, 2005.

Schmid, Alex P., and Jenny de Gaff. *Violence as Communication: Insurgent Terrorism and the Western News Media.* Beverly Hills, CA: Sage Publications, 1982.

BOOKS

Bjorgo, Tore (ed.) *Root Causes of Terrorism.* London: Routledge, 2005.

Buford, Bill. *Among the Thugs.* New York: Norton, 1992.

Gupta, Dipak K. *Path to Collective Madness: A Study in Social Order and Political Pathology.* Westport, CT: Praeger, 2001.

Gupta, Dipak K. *Terrorism and Homeland Security.* Belmont, CA: Wadsworth, 2005.

Mandela, Nelson. *Long Walk to Freedom: The Autobiography of Nelson Mandela.* Boston: Little Brown, 1994.

Rubin, Barry M., and Judith Colp Rubin. *Yasir Arafat: A Political Biography.* New York: Oxford University Press, 2003.

Stern, Jessica. *Terror in the Name of God: Why Terrorists Kill in the Name of God.* New York: Ecco, 2003.

St. John, Warren. *Rammer Jammer Yellow Hammer: A Journey into the Heart of Fan Mania.* New York: Random House, 2004.

Perlmutter, Amos. *The Life and Times of Menachem Begin.* Garden City Park, NY: Doubleday, 1987.

Post, Jerrold M. *Leaders and Their Followers in a Dangerous World: The Psychology of Political Behavior.* Ithaca, NY: Cornell University Press, 2004.

WEBSITES

International Policy Institute for Counter-Terrorism
http://www.ict.org.il

"Patterns of Global Terrorism Report," U.S. State Department
http://www.state.gov/s/ct/rls/pgtrpt

111

DIPAK K. GUPTA is the Fred J. Hansen Professor of World Peace at San Diego State University, Distinguished Professor of Political Science, and Director, International Security and Conflict Resolution (ISCOR). He is the author of six books and over 80 articles. He has been a visiting Fellow at many universities, including the Hoover Institute on War, Revolution, and Peace at Stanford University, St. Antony's College at Oxford University, Leiden University in the Netherlands, and Fudan University in Shanghai. Professor Gupta has lectured in many universities around the world. His primary research areas include various aspects of political violence and terrorism. For further information about Professor Gupta, please visit his home page: http://www-rohan.sdsu.edu/faculty/dgupta/.

The research for this book was funded by a timely grant from the U.S. Institute of Peace.

LEONARD WEINBERG is Foundation Professor of Political Science at the University of Nevada. Over the course of his career he has been a Fulbright senior research fellow for Italy, a visiting fellow at the National Security Studies Center (University of Haifa), a visiting scholar at UCLA, a guest professor at the University of Florence, and the recipient of an H. F. Guggenheim Foundation grant for the study of political violence. He has also served as a consultant to the United Nations Office for the Prevention of Terrorism (Agency for Crime Control and Drug Prevention). For his work in promoting Christian–Jewish reconciliation Professor Weinberg was a recipient of the 1999 Thornton Peace Prize.

WILLIAM L. EUBANK is a graduate of the University of Houston, where he earned two degrees (B.S. and M.A.) in political science. He received his Ph.D. from the University of Oregon in 1978. Before coming to the University of Nevada, he taught briefly at California State University Sonoma and Washington State University. While at the University of Nevada, he has taught undergraduate courses in Constitutional Law, Civil Rights & Liberties, Political Parties and Elections, and graduate seminars in American Politics, the History of Political Science and Research Methods. The author or co-author of articles and papers in areas as diverse as statistics, research design, voting, and baseball, among other subjects, he is interested in how political violence (and terrorism) function as markers for political problems confronting governments.